A VERY SHORT,
FAIRLY INTERESTING AND
REASONABLY CHEAP BOOK ABOUT

BRAND MANAGEMENT

A VERY SHORT, FAIRLY INTERESTING AND REASONABLY CHEAP BOOK ABOUT

BRAND MANAGEMENT

MICHAEL BEVERLAND AND PINAR CANKURTARAN

1 Oliver's Yard
55 City Road
London EC1Y 1SP

2455 Teller Road
Thousand Oaks
California 91320

Unit No 323-333, Third Floor, F-Block
International Trade Tower, Nehru Place
New Delhi 110 019

8 Marina View Suite 43-053
Asia Square Tower 1
Singapore 018960

© Michael Beverland and Pinar Cankurtaran 2025

Apart from any fair dealing for the purposes of research, private study, or criticism or review, as permitted under the Copyright, Designs and Patents Act, 1988, this publication may not be reproduced, stored or transmitted in any form, or by any means, without the prior permission in writing of the publisher, or in the case of reprographic reproduction, in accordance with the terms of licences issued by the Copyright Licensing Agency. Enquiries concerning reproduction outside those terms should be sent to the publisher.

Library of Congress Control Number: 2024944340

British Library Cataloguing in Publication data

A catalogue record for this book is available from the British Library

Editor: Amy Mitchell
Editorial assistant: Maura Mary Joseph
Production editor: Sarah Sewell
Copyeditor: Denver Dominic Willard
Proofreader: Girish Sharma
Indexer: TNQ Tech Pvt. Ltd.
Marketing manager: Elena Asplen
Cover design: Bhairvi Vyas
Typeset by: TNQ Tech Pvt. Ltd.

ISBN 978-1-5297-9517-2
ISBN 978-1-5297-9516-5 (pbk)

[ALSO IN THIS SERIES]

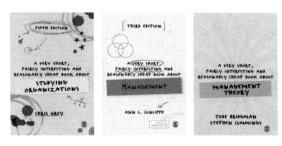

Contents

About the Authors ix

1 Introduction: Studying Brands and Branding 1

2 Past, Present, and Future of Brands and Branding 4
   Where did brands come from? 4
   How have things changed? 7
   What is a brand? 10
   Is everything now a brand? 12
   Who cares about brands? 13
   How has brand management changed? 15

3 The Brand Gurus 19
   Setting the scene 19
   Kevin Lane Keller: customer-based brand equity (CBBE) 20
   David Aaker: strategic insights that resonate through the ages 22
   From psychology to culture: identity as the driver of purchase 23
   Brand communities 25
   Susan Fournier's pioneering work on brand relationships 26
   Consumer Culture Theory (CCT) and brands 30
   Douglas Holt: branding's citizen artist 31
   Practitioner voices 33
   Ehrenberg-Bass: brand science from a land down under 35
   Chapter summary 39

4 How to Speak Like a Branding Pro 40
   How much is that doggie in the window? brand equity and all that 40
   Who are you? the identity issue 43
   Difference, distinction, uniqueness, and parity: what's the difference? 47
   Segments: selling to everyone or selecting a few 52
   Brand audits: can you walk the walk? 55
   Living the brand 57
   Brand research and metrics 61
   Getting to the top of the pyramid: what is all this stuff about awareness, top-of-mind, and salience? 64

	Do you need a brand extension?	67
	Brand architecture: a tale of two houses	68
	Who doesn't love a story? communicating without selling	70
	Keeping it real? what is all the fuss about brand authenticity?	72
	The logo-ism sinners were right all along	76
	Chapter summary	79
5	Enduring Challenges in Branding	80
	Who creates brand meaning?	80
	Art and science, the challenge of scientific laws vs. the creative genius	84
	Relevance and consistency: how to remain forever new, without changing	87
	Can a brand change?	92
	I want to live forever!	96
	Are brands cultural parasites?	98
	Find your purpose! should brands be activists?	101
	Global vs. local	103
	A branded world?	109
	What about the dark arts?	110
	Are brands really (always) about identity? (or, 'I'm not really a brand person')	114
	Do brands make us crazy, or stupid?	116
	Chapter summary	120
6	Epilogue	121

References	125
Index	135

About the Authors

Professor **Michael Beverland** and Associate Professor **Pınar Cankurtaran** are branding and marketing researchers at the University of Sussex Business School. Also responsible for their text *Brand Management: Co-creating Meaningful Brands*, presently in its third edition, the authors have written widely on branding topics including authenticity, innovation, and consumer behavior.

1

Introduction: Studying Brands and Branding

While it's fair to say brands have always fascinated us, our interest in the actual process of branding is more recent. Like most of us, we have our preferred brands, although we often don't know why. We also fill our shopping trolleys (online and off) with a range of preferred brands, yet often have little understanding of why we chose one over the other. We argue vociferously that our brand of beer is better than someone else's, when blind tests typically show that even brand loyalists cannot distinguish their preferred insipid brew from the other mass-market offerings. We have brands that have been with us for years while others come and go, and those we wouldn't admit to owning in polite company. But why is this so? How can we form such a rich array of preferences, often of products and services that are by and large interchangeable with their competitors, without being able to explain why? And what role do marketers play in these outcomes?

Since the turn of the millennium, our interest in brands has moved from consuming them to thinking about how they work, how they're created, changed, and ultimately managed. We've written widely, for a range of audiences, on branding topics from the boringly tactical (how in-store music can impact on brands) to the prosaic (brand authenticity), the strategic (how brands manage stability and change), and the unexpected (how brands can shape images of the nation). We examined brands from a wide array of contexts, from agricultural commodities wanting to brand, to services such as specialty coffee, to luxury products such as fine wine and fashion, through to manufacturing, platforms, and business-to-business. We've advised owners of brands, particularly start-ups (or indeed, re-starts), on how to better communicate their distinctive benefits and stories, how to leverage connections with clients to grow, and how to make rich backstories meaningful to new audiences. We've had the pleasure of meeting some amazing brand marketers, creative professionals, leaders, and fellow brand thinkers. We've taught hundreds of wonderful and not-so-wonderful students, talked to skeptics and believers, and had our fair share of great and terrible experiences from brands.

So after all that, what do we know? First, that branding remains a mix of art and science. Second, that brands and brand managers have far less control than many critics would have us believe. Third, that while consumers may resist, play with, undermine, personalize, or reject brands and their messages, they're just as likely (if not more so) to buy in and play along, for as long as is necessary. Fourth, that our knowledge of brands keeps evolving in a messy, argumentative, and incremental way. Fifth, the scope of what we consider a brand has changed. Brands can involve products and services but also app-based platforms, people, places and popular culture, among others. Sixth, brand claims are subject to more scrutiny than ever, especially when they seek to co-opt culture or take stands on controversial social issues. Finally, despite all we know, debate about the 'best way' to engage in branding remains as fractured and intense as ever—we wouldn't have it any other way.

There are probably more branding experts than there are brands, bringing different degrees of knowledge to debates and coming from different backgrounds, including not only practice and academia but also professions such as marketing, design, creative, finance, advocacy, media, etc., and different sectors. This creates much noise around the subject of branding, numerous beliefs about what works and what doesn't, and multiple fads and fashions, challenges, futures and models. All of this can shape (often irrationally) practice and academic debates, and makes writing a short book about the subject somewhat challenging. But we knew that going in and signed on with Sage anyway.

Over the next hundred or so pages, this guide will provide you insights into some of the enduring debates and controversies in brand management, introduce you to some of the leading thinkers on brands and branding, and unpack as much as possible their respective contributions. If you are in the practitioner game, we will at least help you speak like a brand pro (we know all too well that performativity lies at the heart of modern management) by examining some of the major decisions, ideas, and tools of branding. Finally, we cover some of the enduring and more recent challenges regarding branding, including how one seemingly changes while remaining the same, deals with pesky audiences that want to co-create, goes global, and engages in a higher purpose. We also cover some more troubling aspects of branding, although we also recognize that we may also be providing a blueprint for wannabe despots, drug dealers, and providers of dubious music trends to build their own brands.

On that note, this book is intended to stimulate understanding and debate, as opposed to being a definitive textbook (which, even as authors of such a text, we believe is an impossible goal). While it may guide you in your studies, you will also need other sources to fill in the many gaps herein, stay up-to-date, and build and manage brands. So in marketing parlance consider this short, cheap and (hopefully) fairly interesting guide the first point of the funnel, which, if we whet your appetite may stimulate you to buy our wonderful textbook *Brand Management: Co-creating Meaningful Brands*, that as chance would have it, is also available from the good people at Sage. We do hope though to provide an understanding of brands and branding and some of the key ideas (and their limitations) that shape theory and practice and highlight some of the enduring challenges that define brand management. Mostly, we hope it's not too taxing a read and that you kind of enjoy it (remember this book's title requires to set your expectations accordingly).

2

Past, Present, and Future of Brands and Branding

where did brands come from?

Early on in any of our modules, we usually ask students a simple question – how long has the idea of a brand been around? (Later we ask the same of brand management). It doesn't take long for most to inevitably mumble 'a while'. But how long is 'a while', and since the answer involves thousands of years, why have people felt the need to engage in this practice for so long? The term 'brand' itself dates to the proto-German word *brandr*, which loosely translates to 'burn a mark upon or stigmatize', two often forgotten, sometimes maligned, but still very relevant aspects of branding today that go far beyond an unhealthy obsession with logo design (or 'brand assets' in the parlance of the times). Historians and even archaeologists of branding have traced the practice back to the Early Bronze Age (2250–2000BCE) with identifying marks or 'proto-brands' found on pottery and storage vessels in digs in the Indus Valley (spanning modern day Afghanistan, India, and Pakistan) (Moore and Reid 2008).

These proto brands (defined as such because their symbols often conveyed pragmatic guarantees around origin, quality and transport) evolved over time into forms of branding practice we would be familiar with today, including an emphasis on symbolism, image and personality, and even moral purpose. The famous marks of empires, such as Rome's *SPQR*, reminded citizen and colonized alike of their shared values, place, and of course, that the famed legions were never too far away should one be tempted to develop one's own competitor brand (we're looking at you Vercingetorix). In fact, branding has rather dubious origins. The idea of burning a mark into something usually involved the enslavement of persons, which was then scaled up and perhaps made more insidious (and less physically painful) by empires, eventually becoming all-encompassing brand worlds (what one of the more philosophically-minded consultants we've had the pleasure of sharing a stage with calls a *gesamtkunstwerk* – we believe it means a 'complete world', although we prefer the way the original rolls off the tongue) among the image-minded totalitarian regimes of the 20th century.

On that last point, a slight digression from the historic narrative of heroic marketers pushing back the brand boundaries is in order. Steven Heller's light-hearted coffee table book *Iron Fists: Branding the 20th Century Totalitarian State*, identifies how Fascists and Communists employed many of the tools still in use today for commercial branding in their attempts to achieve total power over citizens and ensure the populace were loyal to the respective regimes. How? Through the design and consistent use of symbols such as the Swastika or Hammer and Sickle, stylized portraits of the regime leaders which seem to never go out of style with politicians (and which were inspiration for the beloved Big Brother in George Orwell's romance novel *1984*), font styles (who can forget the beauty of *Fraktur*), colors, uniforms, manifestos (little red and green books, autobiographical accounts of personal struggles, etc.) and so on. All of these are variants on what today we would call brand assets. Each regime's leading lights acted as Chief Brand Officers (or employed some), exerting control over every aspect of how they were represented across different media channels. Lest culturally-minded brand researchers think they're off the hook, regimes also created brand communities with very distinct in- and out-groups and expected moral standards. These regimes also co-opted cultural sources including the arts, industrial design, sports, and of course other brands, to their cause. The desire for power over subjects is perhaps why we remain somewhat wary of the practitioners of branding's dark arts.

But back to the historical narrative wannabe brand managers like to hear (as researchers on authenticity we know how it important it is for an audience to be given information that confirms their desired identity). During the 19th century, the emergence of tort law in Europe and the United States unintentionally drove firms to invest in their brands. Legal innovations focused on the protection of trademarks and names in emerging market economies. Courts were generally happy to grant the first user of a trading name the right to use that name and to exclude others from using it, particularly within the same product or service category. As markets developed further, firms sought to expand these protections to include the use of symbols, designs, and mascots (Petty 2011). Not all of these were successful, but with the courts being receptive to hearing such claims, marketers continued to push for greater rights to exclusive use of what we would now call brand assets.

Eventually, marketers also began to seek protection for more symbolic, aspirational claims, which the courts largely rejected. Pushing legal boundaries continues to this day, with the marketers at motorcycle-turned-lifestyle brand Harley Davidson seeking to legally protect the supposed distinctive sound of their engine (at the time of writing they have repeatedly failed) and anti-establishment technology brand Apple seeking to own the use of the letter 'i' (which they use on their various products). Such claims generally fail because they are either difficult to distinguish or are seen as part of everyday vocabulary and cannot therefore be owned. These cases no doubt provide the material for novels like Max Barry's *Jennifer Government* where the titular character, a police officer, must take orders from corporate security service representatives with names like John Nike.

Ironically of course, consumers have more recently embraced the idea of a branded subject, using brands to project their desired image to others, with some going so far as to tattoo logos onto their person. Whereas John Carpenter's 1988 satiric film *They Live* warned us of aliens (often dressed as corporate types) using subliminal messages such as 'consume', 'buy more', and 'watch television' to ensure pesky humans remained obedient, street artist Frank Shepard Fairey has, since 2001, turned his 'Obey' artwork into a desirable fashion brand, with its recognizable Orwellian 1984 Big Brother logo worn by rebellious teens globally (in *Matrix* terms, some teens at least prefer the comfort provided by Morpheus' blue pill). As American journalist on consumer culture Rob Walker (2010) argues, consumers are as likely to 'buy in', to embrace brands willingly, openly encouraging marketers to engage in *murketing*, or soft selling via stealth product placement or influencer endorsement.

So what motivates this need to mark stuff to say something about who we are? No doubt there are some pragmatic reasons. Buyers in ancient times were concerned that products they had purchased were in fact the genuine article and had not been adulterated or tampered with (and with shipping times only slightly faster and more reliable than the Royal Mail (in some parts of the UK), returning counterfeit perishables was not an option). Owners could then use these proto brands to earn premiums, shift goods more quickly, build loyalty, and of course enhance their own reputation (an early proxy for brand image). These concerns have not gone away. Subsequently, brands acted as a shortcut for individual product categories (as in Coca cola, or Lux soap), that is they denoted something.

It didn't take long for brands to come to also connote some higher order meaning, such as the nation state, cleanliness, masculinity, luxury, and so on (Levy 1959). For owners, this shift in what brands could mean enabled them to expand beyond narrow functional categories, extend, and even become lifestyle brands. For consumers, the brand now provided a recognizable form of status that could mark them out in terms of identity and membership of a like-minded group of people. And other stakeholders could use the meaning of brands against them, on the assumption that pointing out the distance between their aspirational claims and the reality of their operations would lead brand owners to change their ways.

In a way, trustworthiness, signaling identity and membership are all enduring human needs that, according to writers on postmodern marketing, since the 1990s have been served at least as much by brands as they are by historically-stable markers of individual and collective identity (although this claim seems to have been falsified so often since it was made that one wonders whether markers such as class, race, religion and nation-state were ever de-centered) (Firat and Venkatesh 1995).

how have things changed?

So what can be considered a brand? Recent research and practice suggest that the scope of what we consider a brand has dramatically changed. Whereas proto brands were used to mark products, today, almost everything can be branded. Services, particularly business-to-business ones, used to be above branding, preferring to trade on their reputation. Reputation sounds nicer and is a form of soft branding, because your reputation is something you earn. Branding on the other hand aims to create and shape reputation and is much more proactive as a strategy. Services quickly learned to turn their reputation for something into a brand that promised to do the same, and more. The same goes for place branding.

For academics, with their insatiable desire to build publication pipelines (largely driven by fear and a desperate sense of insecurity), the more 'types' of brands they can identify and pull apart the better. Subfields of branding therefore keep growing, much like unchecked black mold, with the stars of film, music, sport, and television now being classified as specific types of brands. Whereas we once had sitcoms with audiences, now we have serial (as opposed to cereal) brands with engaged communities of fans. Serial brands refer to the idea that unlike the ideal brand that lives forever, TV shows or movie franchises have a distinct start and end date (Russell and Schau 2014). That is until some talentless corporate hack proposes a reboot, at which point they become retro brands (Brown et al. 2003). Confused? We are too.

While politicians of all stripes have certainly used branding, from 20th century totalitarian states to the ubiquitous t-shirts featuring revolutionaries, through to the stylization of a certain look involving a handbag, hairdo, an iron resolve, and possibly a photo in a battle tank, some brands often struggle with links to political regimes (although undoubtedly benefitted from the associations and patronage at the time). Biographies and movies (2024's *The New Look*) of Coco Chanel continue to struggle with her alleged collaboration with the Nazis during the occupation of France. Brands such as Hugo Boss (who designed the SS uniforms), VW, Porsche, BMW, BASF and many more remain tainted by their roles in World War Two (WW2) and the Holocaust. Coca-Cola made a rare misstep when the 75th anniversary of Fanta (which they acquired in 1960) celebrated 'the feeling of the Good Old Times'. Sounds innocent, after all who doesn't love a bit of nostalgia, especially on a major birthday. However, the brand was founded in Nazi Germany during WW2 as the US government had banned the sale of Coca-Cola syrup. Suddenly an appeal to 'the good times' sounds a bit different, and the Fanta team quickly pulled the campaign.

With this strong history in politics and propaganda, you won't be surprised to hear marketing has a subfield of political branding. In the run up to the 2015 UK election, one of your authors was asked to be a spokesperson for his university on branding issues. Turns out there was widespread interest in this approach, and he received more than his entitled 15 minutes of fame (don't worry, obscurity quickly returned, although some would argue the ego never deflated). The media were interested in a range of issues, from the party leaders' fashion choices (the color of ties seems to be a particular fascination among the media, although at least three of the main party leaders were women), the slogans used for campaign launches, the strategies needed by minor brands to cut through, and those needed by the large brands to negate their weak points and appeal to swing voters, who very much reflect the split-loyal consumers that marketers should be appealing to if they wish to grow their market (and if they don't, they may not remain in their roles for long, unless they work in university marketing departments). It also turns out that a brand logic was quite useful for political strategizing too, with clever use of low-emotional content adverts (or ads with no call to action), targeted messaging at swing voters, and staying on-message against a backdrop of opposition in-fighting leading to an unpredicted win for the governing party.

Some things are brands without even knowing it. 'Invisible brands' for example are mundane everyday items such as baking soda, cleaners, ingredients and so on that we take for granted, but according to academics, are actually incredibly powerful because they signal an identity of being a proper homemaker (Coupland 2005). Lest you think we're being harsh on academics, it's fair to say there are also a whole range of professionals and professional cranks who offer advice to unsuspecting clients. Expertise, or the appearance of it, can be easily accessed to help turn your nation, your region, your city, or even a neighborhood into a brand. Who after all can forget such gems as the 'C U in the NT' (NT being Northern Territory) or 'Where the bloody hell are you' from those geniuses of Australian place branding? Kiwis also get in on the act with their award winning 100% Pure (which the Guardian recoined as 98% pure bullshit) while the first author's personal favorite is for dairy town Hamilton whose put-upon local taxpayers actually shelled out for 'More than you'd expect' (believe us, it was from a low base and still missed the mark).

Whereas stars used to be talent, the giants of modern pop such as Rihanna and Justin Timberlake now act as brands, extending their name onto a range of goods such as beauty and fragrance (Fenty, in the case of Rihanna) and also extending their franchises into different sectors such as film and television, much to the chagrin of their record companies who are desperate for some new releases that actually have the power to shift millions in an age where streaming has decimated the occurrence of diamond, platinum and gold albums. Celebrity brands of rap artists even get into fights or record songs known as 'diss tracks' aimed at trashing their imagined opponent. The most famous of this is the fight that occurred after the breakup of West Coast pioneers NWA (Ice Cube's 'No Vaseline' doesn't need much interpretation). These often-staged rivalries actually enhance the communal bonds surrounding each act, as having at least an imagined rival is central to what we call brand communities – that's right, even groups of fans are now branded.

Some CEOs and indeed designers and other professionals are so well known that their return to (or departure from) a company can enhance the brand. The likes of Steve Jobs, Miuccia Prada, Howard Schultz and Anna Wintour are all brands who enhance and benefit from associations with other brands. One seminal study of person-brands used the idea of the 'two-bodies' to understand the difficulty firms have when their CEO's or founders transcend celebrity status and become brands. Susan Fournier and Giana Eckhardt (2019) examined Martha Stewart, the once-loved (at least by the middle classes) homemaker, until she found herself facing criminal charges and jail time for some share trading anomalies.

The two-bodies challenge is an old idea that refers to the management of royalty – one body is temporal, subject to human problems and ultimately mortality, whereas the other body, the crown, is enduring (until the people get sick of the whole thing and remove both bodies – don't worry aspiring royals, the surviving royal families are some of the best brand franchisers going). A brand like Stewart is powerful because of her personal authenticity and investment in the brand, but for those shareholders in the company, this also presents risks. Apple's loss of co-founder Steve Jobs to ill health did result in an initial write-down of the brand's value (which it has since recovered). No one quite knows the brand like the founder, and consumers prefer to connect with aspirational figureheads than more abstract ideals (which is why royal brands put a lot of emphasis on humanizing their senior members). But founders, such as Martha Stewart, can do wrong, and then what happens to the brand? Turns out, it loses value. Which is why owners try and manage two-bodies, slowly disassociating the enduring brand body from the mortal and possibly problematic person-brand body. It's not an easy task, as most brands do not enjoy the constitutional protections that royalty do.

However, we can go further – you yourself can be a brand. In the 2010 season of serial brand *The Apprentice*, one contestant went so far as to refer to himself as 'the brand'. Turns out the hardened senior manager charged with judging this contestant's character wasn't convinced and 'the brand's' run ended quite quickly after that. But anyway, in 1997, serially flip-flopping person-brand Tom Peters told wannabe tech bros (he was writing in *Fast Company*) to 'be the brand called you', and triggered a whole industry of personal brand consultants, life coaches, and job mentors. These professionals often take some basic principles of brand tactics that make sense (such as having a concise and interesting elevator pitch about your skills), and with the help of social media platforms, push you to be a brand. Thereafter you focus on curating content, which usually involves sharing the same aspirational fluff as everyone else (and quickly loses you followers).

There is of course a required tone of voice for such brands, with authenticity only arising from endless claims of extreme humility as well as pride for your pseudo achievements (in academia this results in claims of joining particular 'clubs', usually based on arbitrary citation cut-offs). Or you can be bashful, claim to have invented whole words, and a reputation based on a thin CV of achievements and go on to lead your country, regardless of any questionable associations in your past (not mentioning any specific reality TV person-brands here for fear we'll be labeled 'fake news').

what is a brand?

Such a simple question, but one that has resulted in many different answers over the years. Smarter minds that us (although we too have attempted it, largely to chase citations) have attempted to define what a brand actually is, as opposed to the constituent parts of a brand (signs and symbols) or even the outcomes of branding (a point of difference relevant to the target user). Definitions have proliferated over the years as different functional domains have become interested in branding. The target audience for a particular definition also matters, with those aimed at CEO's differing from those targeting the design profession for example. Finally, as academic knowledge about brands and branding have developed, updates to official or authoritative definitions have occurred. So what is a brand?

Early on, David Aaker (1991) proposed that a brand was a range of symbols that helped distinguish your market offering from that of competitors. Such a definition left out the consumers of that brand and certainly accorded them no co-creative role in its meaning. Aaker was of course a pioneer, and while it's easy to criticize those who came first for what they left out, his approach did suggest that one could compete symbolically (at a time when people were focused on quality – price trade-offs) and that one needed to be positioned differently from competitors. Aaker's audience was primarily CEO's, who are less concerned with a brand means to a consumer and more concerned with how to survive and thrive in competitive environments. Despite its limitations, it was a good start and one that made branding a strategic concern rather than a more tactical communications focus (plus, Aaker is one of those lovely academic-practitioners who constantly updates their thinking as they learn more).

However, with its focus on symbolic differentiation, this definition did have the unfortunate effect of equating brands with their logos, which suggested that brand consumption was relatively meaningless and driven solely by image. Subsequent definitions have attempted to remedy this, often by bringing in the consumer as a generator of brand meaning or as, at the very least, the receiver of the brand's supposed benefits. While examining multiple definitions of branding is beyond this short guide, there does seem to be some enduring features of brand definitions that are worth considering. First, brands identify origin either directly or through some set of distinct brand assets such as logos. Second, brands seek to differentiate the offers of one entity from another. Third, to this end they should be distinctive enough to legally protect. Fourth, brands are carriers of meaning. Fifth, brands are valued for something, by someone. That is, they must meet a need. Sixth, brands are generally experienced through use. With all that in mind we define brands as:

> An intangible, symbolic marketplace resource, imbued with meaning by stakeholders and the broader context in which it is embedded, that enables users to project their identity goal(s) to one or more audiences. (Beverland and Cankurtaran 2024 p. 10)

The definition above seems far away from the simple elegance of David Aaker's starting point, but we believe it also reflects how research has changed our understanding of brands and branding over time. We retain the focus on a symbolic asset as a means of competing and adding value to users, while introducing an emphasis on multiple meaning creators through reference to stakeholders and the wider context of use (which includes market systems, subcultures, nations, and so on). We then stress the importance of identity goals and explain how they underpin much, if not all, brand consumption and of course also reflect the desire of the organization to create a branded identity in the marketplace.

Defining a brand is a moving target, often reflecting particular disciplinary perspectives, target audiences or points in time. No doubt someone will find fault with our definition, we'd be surprised if they didn't (although we would spite you for some time). We may even tire of it ourselves. But for now, let's run with it (and if you don't like it, have a go yourself).

is everything now a brand?

As well as all these different types of brands, there are other points of confusion. We've often been asked, is a supermarket a brand, or simply a place that sells brands? The answer is of course both. In fact, smart supermarkets may even have their own brands, sometimes called retailer brands, buyers' own brands, house brands, or own labels. Some might even be branded as a retailer brand, such as Marks and Spencer (M&S) range of products; while others may appear as distinct brands in store but are in fact own brands to provide the appearance of choice, such as Autograph (by M&S). In fact, retailers are often quite good at buying dying brands such as Ted Baker (the brand started to flounder after it was alleged that its founder had a propensity to offer unwanted hugs to his staff) or the ethically-minded Body Shop, reducing their clutter, and using them to enhance their product range.

Retailers use their own brands for a number of reasons. First, it trades on their own equity. Second, it means they can capture more value, and keep the other brands in line. For example, Tesco will stock Coke and Pepsi of course, but also their own-brand cola (probably made by one of the other two), largely as a power play. Third, customers often are quite loyal to retail stores, especially when they have to drive to do a weekly shop and can be positively disposed towards own brands. Finally, own brands often can reduce cost because they share the marketing with the retailer brand and are therefore useful strategically for retailers seeking to offer lower prices because they're just really nice, or more likely, to fend off discounters.

There are other hierarchies of brands. Firms may organize brands in a variety of ways. There may be an organization that has many brands (we call this a 'house of brands'), or an organization that *is* the brand (what we call a 'branded house'), or hybrids. Some organizations may also have a brand for different stakeholders. Consider luxury behemoth Louis Vuitton Moët Hennessey, or LVMH if you're into the whole brevity thing. This group owns a vast array of brands, and retail stores which are also brands and often have their own brand ranges (Sephora for example). Yet, LVMH does not make anything at all. The group brand is how the stock is listed on the exchange and is of course targeted at shareholders who buy LVMH stocks because of how all those other brands perform. We will cover this more when we discuss something called brand architecture.

The key thing to keep in mind is brands are simply tools for organizations. How a firm may organize its brand structure may reflect a variety of things, including history, the role of each brand, the strength of individual brands vs. the group, whether one brand can be stretched to new uses or associations, and so on. We shouldn't get too hung up on brands, nor treat them with too much respect. When streamlining makes sense, then it should be encouraged, but if consumer research suggests it won't, then you need to move more slowly.

who cares about brands?

Turns out quite a lot of folks. But still, you may ask, why? For many reasons. For organizations they're treated as an intangible asset (although whether they fit the definition of asset is debatable), which potentially enhances the value of the firm in the eyes of shareholders (with over 80% of listed stocks comprising intangible value at the time of writing). This valuation in part flows from the belief (again contestable) that loyalty has lifetime value, that is, it will generate discounted cash flows over time. There are many benefits of brands for organizations that we will touch on in the rest of this guide, but studies have shown brands earn a price premium, and also make sales and growth easier. As we will also discuss, brands can also be grown via an extension of their meaning, into new price points or usage scenarios, or even new categories and markets.

For consumers the picture is more mixed. Undoubtedly brands do matter, but the question is 'how much?' Historically, brands were viewed as simple devices that conveyed information and resulted in trust. Later on we added even more meaning and knowledge, but still tended to focus on advantages, usually performance-based. As we will see in the next chapter, socioculturally-oriented researchers identify that brands may mean an immense amount to consumers... until they don't.

Postmodernist writers note that in an age defined by hyperreality (or an age where images dominate) and the de-centering of traditional markers of identity such as nation state, religion, class, and ethnicity (although history has a way of messing with this idea, often with devastating consequences) (Firat and Venkatesh 1995), brands can provide imagined community or at least shared meaning (Cayla and Eckhardt 2008). Brands are seen as open to all (unless they chose not to be) and less divisive (until they become activists) and therefore useful for communicating desired identity, both at the individual and collective level.

Some authors, including us, have even gone so far as to argue brands can provide the basis for restoring a sense of national identity, although they seem far less able to tackle national problems such as inequality, a sense of exclusion, and climate change (among other things) (Beverland et al. 2021). Others have noted how consumers can use local brands to reject globalization or twist the meaning of global brands cleverly for nationalist purposes (Dong and Tian 2009). Still others identify how even everyday brands that were once hated and, in some cases, been long dead, have now been revived to provide a nostalgic salve for collective hurt (Brunk et al. 2018). Brands seem to be anything but simple, especially when clever academics adopt them as a lens to craft the 'theoretical contribution' so essential to their fame and distinction.

As we will see in the next chapters, others say 'not so fast'. suggesting that brands don't matter that much to consumers, or at least consumers can't really tell them apart from one another, and eventually lose interest, switching their loyalties to another, before sending their new best friend packing (Sharp 2010). Clearly, brands matter to consumers and by extension business buyers, although one can argue about why and how much.

In the final chapter we will examine other benefits of brands, many of which are more dubious. When one talks about nation or person-brands it is important to not equate useful branding strategies to communicate with investors and tourists and followers with the logic of branding per se. People are far more interesting than brands, and certainly more and more residents of jam-packed cities are fighting back against place branding (whose practitioners seemed to have forgotten the importance of differentiation or distinction to brands). Furthermore, branding as a practice can be used by legitimate as well as, shall we say, more legally or morally questionable operators. And the unintended, but after all this time, not improbable consequences of branding are all too often rarely considered.

how has brand management changed?

When we teach branding in our MBA classes we need to skip over history, and usually theory, fairly quickly, lest we be framed immediately as out-of-touch academics by our students who often have the benefit of at least 18 months of in-house 'work' experience via their graduate program. We joke of course. Actually the niggle in MBA classes where you need to provide your relevance credentials is kind of fun and not a bad thing for us ivory tower folk to experience once in a while. After a couple of slides of potted history which we have covered earlier in this chapter, we find it useful to show two slides of seminal book titles about brand management – one from the foundational years of the 1990s and one from the 21st century. If students are still with us (and not hogging the so-called free food they love), then they will note that the implied assumptions about who controls the brand has changed, as have beliefs about how to manage for meaning successfully. Since we have a minimum word count to hit for Sage, then let's do the same exercise here.

The original books of branding in the 1990s all had titles such as *Strategic Brand Management* (Keller 2003) and *Managing Brand Equity* (Aaker 1991), both of which left one in no doubt who controlled the brand and how it was managed. Brands were assets to be carefully managed by brand managers, with little room for the consumer or anyone else for that matter. Make no mistake, these books are classics, and deserve to be on the shelf of any aspiring brand manager, but they come from a time when the focus of brand management was making sure that received brand image (by the audience) was the same as intended brand identity (by the organization). Consumers who acted in ways contrary to what marketers wanted, and these could include failing to fit within desired target markets or using the brand in unintended ways, could even find themselves threatened with legal action. LEGO for example threatened its adult fans with cease-and-desist letters because these consumers had the temerity to continue to use the brand long after the suggested age range. Consider that during this time the brand that eventually became defined by 'creativity at play' was nearing bankruptcy, as children found electronic games far more exciting that plastic bricks and blocky character figures. The brand was literally suing the only customers it had, and these customers often bought up big (Beverland 2009).

One classic example of this comes from what became known as the corporate branding field. Mary Jo Hatch and Majken Schultz's (2001) groundbreaking work came with titles such as 'Are the strategic stars aligned for your corporate brand?' The accompanying 2008 book subtitled 'How companies can align strategy, culture, and identity through corporate branding' says it all. Their focus is on managing for gaps between how employees see the brand and their promise to customers, the image customers and stakeholders have of the brand, and the desired brand image of the firm. Gaps are to be tracked and closed, in order for the organization to speak with one consistent, authentic voice. Although their work is very much open to the idea that different images of the brand can exist, it also reinforces the dominant logic of the time – the role of brand managers was to remove the reasons for these gaps in the first place.

This emphasis on consistency of expression, tone, and action remains critical to brand management to this day. Brands are communicative devices and inconsistencies can lead to confusion. But they also reflect a largely economic logic of ownership, whereby the firm controls the brand and in effect tells the consumer (and any stakeholders) what it is for. There is a danger of forgetting the other part of the brand equity equation (which we shall explore throughout the book), psychological ownership. A brand's equity or value is based partly on the strength of relationship the customer has with it. They may not own the brand in the economic sense, but the brand manager's job is to create some felt ownership for it in the emotional sense. This is what makes the non-target groups of consumers such as adult Lego fans, hardy Apple fans in the doldrum 1990s, and wannabe rebels who kept riding Harley Davidsons, continue to hold out hope that the brand will return their love.

We said two comparative slides, so let's get to the second one. Apart from shamelessly plugging the first author's own book on brand authenticity (which due to its massive success you can no longer buy), we show a range of books with titles like *Brand Hijack* (Wipperfürth 2005), *Join the Conversation* (Jaffe 2007), *Citizen Brand* (Gobé 2010), and *Brand Jam* (Gobé 2007). What has changed here? Partly (the then newly-emergent) social media made more apparent the ways in which brands could be parodied, mashed up, used in different ways (Coke as toilet cleaner for example), and used to build communities around. Also, some brands, largely written off even by their own marketing teams were often revived through unexpected uses, users, or communities. And some big-time flops, such as Quaker Oats' purchase of rebellious Snapple were attributed to the failure to understand the meaning of the brand to its users (long-time fan and unassuming radio host Howard Stern renamed the brand 'Crapple' in response to Quaker's desire to remove it's supposed quirks) (Deighton 1999).

What was the message of this new wave of brand writers? In essence, they told brand managers to lighten up. Control over brand image was neither achievable nor desirable. Brand meaning always involved at least two, and often more, partners. Brands were not something done to consumers but were co-created with them. With marketers suggesting that brands had symbolic meaning, it should not surprise that consumers and others may run with that practice, with unexpected effects. Their new metaphors all captured a more ground-up approach to brand management that should resonate with fans of Henry Mintzberg's emphasis on aligning emergent and planned strategy as a more realistic approach to value creation (Mintzberg and Waters 1985).

Take hijacks for example. Fashion brands have always attempted to signal some type of status, whether it be wealth, membership, or values. But this opens them up to being hijacked by those who desire to be part of the club they feel shut out of, or to be reworked, often by new cultural influencers. This can be undesired by the brand (such as the adoption of Burberry's famous plaid patterned cap by 'chavs', a subgroup of lower socioeconomic class consumers in the UK) or revive the brand. Brands such as Ralph Lauren and Tommy Hilfiger in the USA had always drawn on upper-class preppy culture to appeal to mass markets. However, this image was overwhelmingly WASP (white Anglo-Saxon Protestant), which was having a waning influence on the all-important teen market. When African American rappers in effect co-opted these symbols of white success to signal their own cultural power, they gained a newfound level of cool with white consumers, driving their relevance and sales. Old brand theorists would have advised caution, but 21st century branding simply abided and went with the flow.

Whereas simply allowing a brand to be hijacked by anyone can have a number of downsides (changed image, negative associations, and so on, which led Burberry to remove their famous cap from the UK market for a period of time), the other metaphors offer a more nuanced version of co-creation. The idea of citizen brands in many ways harks back to a much earlier period when paternalistic capitalists tried to use their wealth for the betterment of society ('better' from their point of view, at least). Like citizens, brands have responsibilities as well as rights. To be seen as legitimate, a citizen brand must align with social norms that may be subcultural or even wider. Such as idea has been picked up by the likes of Douglas Holt (2002) (covered in the next chapter) who suggests brand managers must be citizen artists, who aim to contribute to community in order to earn the right to profit from it.

Perhaps the idea of 'jam' best captures the shift in meaning management that has occurred in the social media era. For the nonmusical among you, a jam involves several musicians playing off one another, and although initially it is a mess, eventually the players start to synchronize, and a new tune emerges that represents more than sum of its parts. With fragmented communication channels, multiple segments, disparate social movements, and a multitude of meanings attached to the same the brand (as a result of individualized brand relationships; see Fournier next chapter), brand meaning management is increasingly like being in a jam, or at least being a conductor of a very experimental orchestra.

We will cover the issue of who controls the brand and the role of a brand manager in a more emergent, ever-changing landscape later. For now, we will leave it at saying that managing a brand is more difficult than ever, especially in times of greater competition, global expansion, technological disruption, and shifting consumer loyalty. What a brand is and how it is managed will forever be in flux, a situation reflected in the next chapter which focuses on the intellectual evolution of brand management knowledge.

3

The Brand Gurus

setting the scene

At the core of a successful brand lies the contested concept of loyalty. We say contested because how loyalty is built and more importantly how valuable it actually is (if at all) has framed almost every approach to brand management since the early 1990s. Whereas economists often treated brands as carriers of information which helped make markets more efficient, it was the deregulation of many financial markets in the 1980s that drove an interest in how brands came to be valuable. Triggered by Australian media mogul Rupert Murdoch deciding to break with accounting tradition and list brands as assets on his balance sheet, the subsequent buying up in the United Kingdom and the United States of established names at stratospheric prices (or in financial parlance, 'multiples' that were not justified by the acquired firm's stock of tangible assets) led to calls for a scientific approach to branding.

Why? Well for accounting purposes, brands had previously been treated as reputation or goodwill that for tax reasons had to be written off (in the United Kingdom very quickly). This reduced the profits of businesses run by corporate raiders, which in turn made them vulnerable to like-minded others. Brand-driven businesses such as Unilever and Procter & Gamble were also felt to be undervalued, as most of their value was tied up in their hundreds of protected brand names rather than in fixed assets. Corporate raiders recognized that far from being a liability to write down, loyalty to the brand was an asset that could enhance the balance sheet and controversially, be revalued upwards (Power 1992). This led them to often pay a multiple or premium way above what share market analysts thought reasonable to acquire the company. The treatment of a brand as an asset made sense (at least to share traders), however, academics and practitioners had no framework to guide them on how the loyalty that underpinned that asset was built.

Fortunately, people were stepping forward with their take on how brands can be managed effectively long before vacuous feel-good inspiring TED Talks came about (much like nature, grift thought leadership abhors a vacuum).

While there are a number of extremely influential and great writers on branding, the next sections will review those who have had more enduring relevance or impact. We will start with two of the so-called 'fathers of modern branding': David Aaker and Kevin Lane Keller. To answer the problem of brand valuation that emerged in the 1980s–1990s, the Marketing Science Institute (MSI) in the United States (made up of leading practitioners and academics) listed brand valuation as a research priority and funded several conferences and projects on this problem. Rising academic star Kevin Lane Keller (1993) responded to the call and generated a framework to guide research and practice. Keller, along with David Aaker, had built his reputation on understanding brand extension, or how one exploits the value of an existing brand by transferring it somewhere else. With the psychological turn in marketing in full swing, they argued that extensions worked when the parent brand and new extension 'fit' together. By implication they were putting consumer decision making, and importantly, loyal consumers at the center of managing brands.

Kevin Lane Keller: customer-based brand equity (CBBE)

Keller's Customer-based Brand Equity (CBBE) framework was given pride of place as the lead article in the prestigious *Journal of Marketing* in 1993. The CBBE focused on understanding how brands came to be valued in the eyes of the customer, with the implication that the strength of their loyalty would somehow drive financial valuation. Drawing together best practice and academic research, Keller presented, in pyramid form (writers on brands love geometric shapes, including hexagons and, in the case of French brand pioneer Jean Noël Kapferer (2012), prisms) a model in which brand equity was built in a step-by-step fashion, through deepening the consumer's knowledge of what the brand was for, what made it special, how it delivered, and ultimately how it was perceived as unique or special. The more you know about a brand, the more you love it, assuming you like what you know.

Keller's model therefore stresses the ways in which knowledge is built, by emphasizing the dual tools of brand identity and brand image. Brand identity is what we desire as brand managers the brand to be. This is often called the intended brand identity, and it simply reflects all the decisions we have made around positioning (which we cover in the next chapter) and how that is to be expressed in the market. So Nike for example desire that their brand be seen as something that enables personal empowerment through sport, which is expressed, simply and memorably (like all good positions), as 'if you have a body, you are an athlete'. Now that's not too snappy for the market, but the slogan 'Just Do It!' captures the intended identity perfectly (and can be leveraged across multiple media channels).

Brand image on the other hand is how the customer or intended audience sees the brand. Obviously, you'd like them to be in sync, and this is why you track your key associations to see if your target audience is getting the message. The reality is messier, but Keller's framework aims for alignment by ensuring that customers understand what associations the brand has. These associations include attributes of the offer, an array of functional, symbolic and experiential benefits, and a general favorability rating. In the CBBE framework, it is ultimately these image factors that help strengthen the relationship of the customer to the brand.

Keller's model, or variations on it, effectively represents the dominant model that guides practice and even much academic research to this day. Even vociferous critics of CBBE cannot really escape it (Holt 2004), acknowledging the model's dominance among academics and practitioners, while those who proffer alternatives are for the most part flattering via counterfeiting. Criticism or even challenges are shrugged off by Keller (2023) with good cheer, as he often reframes these alternatives as simply new forms of knowledge that slot nicely within his framework. CBBE has also created its own industry, sitting ultimately at the heart of many financial valuation tools, but also providing bread-and-butter consulting to market research agencies who engage in annual brand tracking, where they attempt, through tools that measure conscious and subconscious awareness, how much the consumer knows and likes about the brand (do they know it at all, do they know it if they see it, do they know without seeing it, do they mention it first and so on).

Other psychological theories, often of more dubious value, followed. For decades, practitioners such as J. Walter Thompson (JWT) had sold brands by featuring ideal consumers in their ads. Drawing on personality theory, they had attempted to make brands aspirational to a growing middle class from the 1950s onward. While useful as a communications tool for consumers suffering from status anxiety, some began to wonder if consumers would actually attribute human characteristics to a brand. In 1997, Jennifer Aaker (daughter of the famous David) developed a brand personality scale, arguing that certain types of brands were viewed as personalities reflected in five dimensions: outdoor brands were rugged, ethical brands sincere, luxury brands sophisticated, creative brands exciting, and reliable brands competent. Brand personality is much criticized, partly because personality is loosely defined, and partly because of issues around measures including the validity of the dimensions, the cultural transferability of the scale, and the completeness of it. Jungian psychologists breathed life into this concept by suggesting that brands could embody archetypes such as trickster, earth mother, and so on. The overuse (or perhaps thoughtless use) of such ideas in practice has led to a backlash. While such concepts may be useful for thinking about your target consumer or even the tone of voice for the brand's communications, many question whether consumers really see brands in human form or whether concepts such as personality are as stable as first thought.

David Aaker: strategic insights that resonate through the ages

David Aaker also released his seminal works around this time, including the tightly written *Managing Brand Equity* (1991), which provided a more practical pathway into creating, managing and growing brands. Although it is very much written for the time-poor marketer, the book is rich in insights and despite its age should remain on the essential reading list for brand managers. The book echoes much of the work he and Keller did together and represented one of the first genuine guidebooks on strategic brand management. The book was a runaway bestseller, and resulted in a stream of follow up books, including *Building Strong Brands* (1996) and *Brand Leadership* (2000) among many others. Despite his successes and stature, Aaker always updates his work in light of evidence, which is one of the reasons for his enduring relevance. His agency Prophet was one of the first to champion the importance of relevance and authenticity in branding, which are critical to brand growth.

Aaker's greatest insights, at least for us, stem from his strategic focus. Whereas Keller focuses on understanding and enhancing the consumer's relationship with the brand (which is of course essential), Aaker's focus is more on strategic pathways to sustainable growth. In *Brand Leadership*, Aaker and co-author Erich Joachimsthaler focused on the organizational support structures essential for sustaining equity growth. This echoes back to Procter & Gamble's pre-WW2 'brand management system' which restructured the organization around separate brands, and literally created little fiefs run by powerful brand managers (who were still subject to a ruthless internal rate-of-return logic which could see them dethroned or welcomed to the goody room pretty quickly). This system enabled brand managers to focus purely on their brand, contracting directly with advertising agencies, building their own teams, launching new products, and being accountable to head office for growth. By the late 1980s this system was the norm across many sectors within the United States and beyond (Low and Fullerton 1994). Aaker updated this, blending his insights in brand architecture (portfolio management), with widespread understanding of brand positioning (predating much work on internal branding) and a focus on innovation.

With the revival of Apple in the 2000s, Aaker returned to his original interest in extension but elevated it to a strategic principle. Aaker (2012) identified how Apple had disrupted sectors through the development of new categories (tablets, smartphones, iPod, iTunes) and then essentially disrupted itself, cannibalizing its own categories with better devices. While Apple deliberately killed its brand-saving iPod, other companies were quickly rushing out with their own variants, reinforcing their follower identity while commentators discussed at length Apple's latest breakthrough product. This not only worked for sales and returns, but critically, framed the brand as a leader and it was this image that created so much loyalty and hype within the market. Rather than category extensions as a pathway to growth, Aaker argued that creative destruction was very much the way to enhance brand image to drive relevance. This is perhaps why many financial brand measures continue to rate technology brands highly in terms of value, often in spite of their size (in 2023 disruptive e-vehicle pioneer Tesla was valued higher than the world's largest automotive company Toyota for this very reason).

At the time of writing, Aaker was championing brand purpose (2022), or the focus on higher order goals (as opposed to social causes) for enduring relevance. We will cover this later in the final chapter.

from psychology to culture: identity as the driver of purchase

While Keller and his colleagues were operating within the mainstream of academic writing, a fringe group of researchers were beginning to question the orthodox view that consumers were akin to information processors. Known as the epistemology wars in academic marketing, scholars lined up on the qualitative–quantitative divide and, according to those who were there (way before our time), actually threw chairs at one another, and fought for (or resisted) change. One of the earliest advocates for plurality, Russell Belk gave talks in which he took orthodox marketing assumptions about consumer motivation to their logical end point, forcing attendees at his seminars (which he took on an extensive road show) to openly admit they viewed consumers as robots (it helped that Belk was a trained and published psychology-oriented academic of some standing).

Belk and like-minded academics such as Elizabeth Hirschman, Bernard Cova, Grant McCracken, Linda Price, Morris Holbrook, and others either drew on backgrounds in anthropology and cultural studies or were motivated to study areas such as collecting, boycotts, and other activities that involved consumers but were ignored by mainstream marketing research. They saw consumer research as a separate academic domain from marketing management, with consumer behavior worthy of theoretical consideration as an end in itself (which is always helpful for opening up new avenues in academic research, thereby creating new career opportunities) (Arnould and Thompson 2005). What this meant in practice was that although consumer insights could have managerial value, academically they did not need to. Some lament that this split has had a negative effect, while others identify how over time the two fields have come back together.

Funded by the Marketing Science Institute USA, Belk and ethnographers John Sherry Jr. and Melanie Wallendorf (1989) hit the road in what would become a famous Winnebago and undertook a consumer odyssey (that for its members certainly felt like ten years). Captured on hours of video tape (which remain as an open archive, albeit largely ignored, for scholars to view), the three authors filmed interviews (vox pop and more formal structured depth interviews), along with behavior at a range of places where consumers congregated. Unlike the titular character in Homer's Odyssey, Belk and friends were neither seduced by sirens nor banished by a vengeful god for ten years, but they did learn much from their extensive journey across the United States. The consumer odyssey tried to capture the lived experience of consumers and was responsible for producing several highly cited papers that would eventually form the basis for what became institutionalized (by Arnould and Thompson in 2005) as consumer culture theory.

How does this matter for branding? The two most important insights were that consumers used brands to reflect their real or desired self (or indeed *selves*), and that they were active meaning-makers. Whereas brand promises had largely been focused on functional performance appeals, those writing in what eventually became a cultural tradition identified that consumption was driven heavily by identity concerns. Whereas Keller's model, despite its name, saw the consumer as primarily a passive recipient of brand marketing materials, cultural writers argued consumers were active meaning creators and could contest desired brand identity (which gave rise to the need to track brand image and, more recently, engagement and sentiment among consumers). Furthermore, consumers were both generative of culture and influenced by it, both of which had implications for brand image and brand management.

brand communities

Once the ethnographers formed an admittedly small beachhead in the top academic journals, a new generation of researchers began to make inroads into brand management. Two studies in particular had a major influence on theory and practice. The first involved John and Jim (Schouten and McAlexander respectively) donning leathers and heading out with other weekend warriors to understand the enduring consumer attraction (but failing market power) of the Harley Davidson motorcycle. Both were anthropologists and wondered if consumers also formed social bonds with one another and if this could be commercially valuable. Turns out it was, and the brand was being kept alive by numerous, and often competing, tribes of riders, all of whom saw the brand as a symbol of rebellion and escape. Those who felt emasculated in white collar roles five days a week, donned leathers and rode fat bikes in the weekend to reclaim their manhood. Female riders usurped the ultimate symbol of masculinity, forcing male passengers to 'ride bitch'. This brand community was made up of a range of distinct subcultures with names such as Star of Davidson (for Jewish riders), Dykes on Bikes (lesbian riders), and even racist nationalist groups. Although in theory many of these groups shared little in common in terms of their values and lifecycles, what they did share was the brand, or more importantly, the brand's symbolic meaning (Schouten and McAlexander 1995).

It turned out that whereas managers of the brand had cut costs and tried to make bikes more like their Japanese counterparts, consumers saw the brand as representing an American tradition forged in masculinity, freedom, and the outlaw spirit. These insights helped the new management team to reposition Harley Davidson as a lifestyle brand, leveraging the rebellious spirit of its consumers to sell non-riders branded jackets, key rings, and even fragrance. Being representative of a lifestyle meant the team could leverage their communal associations, and practically meant they were not reliant on one-off purchases of expensive motorcycles. The notion of brand community was born and has since seen a range of firms walk the fine line between their economic ownership of the brand and their consumers' psychological ownership of its meaning, generating community get togethers, on- and off-line outings, crowdsourcing innovations and so on.

A plethora of research followed, examining the ways in which brands can benefit from being part of subculture (Kates 2004), demonstrating how fleeting tribes can see some brands go viral (Canniford 2011), often with results that are not always desired by managers (including the adoption of non-target consumer groups such as those aligned with the political far right), and placing an emphasis on how brands co-create meaning in communal contexts (Schau et al. 2009). This last part is difficult for brand managers used to their command-and-control approaches to meaning, as being successful within a communal space requires giving up some control over meaning creation as well as the process of branding itself. Research has also identified that any communal approach must put community at the heart of the brand's strategy, rather than just see it in tactical terms (Fournier and Lee 2009).

Community has often also been at the heart of attempts by a range of innovators who engage with what academics call 'liquid consumption models' (which, counter-intuitively, have little to do with the beverages). A new wave of platform brands, such as those offering ridesharing and access-based services have attempted to create communality among consumers, with little success. These platforms desire communality to ensure rented bikes and scooters are returned in good condition and to areas that others can easily access, while also trying to create a subculture of smart nomads who are not wasting money on owning things they hardly use, as well as being more sustainable (although studies have noted how dubious many of these claims are) (Bardhi and Eckhardt 2017). Consumer culture researchers have unpicked these models and noted that the immateriality at the heart of platform brands' espoused benefits reduces our connection to things, making us less sustainable (for example, we now use ride-sharing services when we would have once walked, taken public transport or indeed not traveled at all). Perhaps less paradoxically, it also makes us less connected to things, encouraging more of a throwaway culture in the pursuit of convenience on demand (Beverland et al. 2022).

Susan Fournier's pioneering work on brand relationships

In Boston, Susan Fournier had begun to wonder if consumers formed relationships with brands. This may sound weird, but at the time marketing scholarship and practice were undergoing a relational turn as they sought to exploit the value of long-term customers (the mantra of 'it's easier to sell to an existing customer than acquire a new one' was common at the time), usually through customer relationship management (CRM) software.

Fournier (1998) however argued that all too often, relationships were something managers did to customers rather than something they had with them. Fournier undertook multiple long-form (or 'life') interviews with three consumers in her mega-cited article 'Consumers and their brands: Developing relationship theory in consumer research' to explore in-depth the relationships consumers formed with the brands in their lives. She examined multiple brands for each consumer, a fact often forgotten by those who dismiss her research as being from a small sample (the sample size of brands was 112, plus she also quantified her results in her PhD dissertation) and found that consumers had an array of relationships with brands, such as 'best friend', to 'abusive partner', 'secret affairs', 'flings', and many others.

These relationships were of different intensities and durations and ranged from positive to negative. Fournier is a great marketer and therefore knows the power of a 2 × 2 matrix. Relationships were therefore modeled on the x-axis in terms of their intensity (from weak to strong) and on the y-axis in terms of their purpose (from emotional to functional). For example, for one consumer, their favorite sports team was thought of as their second spouse: an intense and largely emotional relationship. Whereas a toothpaste brand was more like a casual acquaintance: the relationship was weak and largely functional. There were interesting combinations too. A fling for example was emotional and intense, but obviously shorter lived than a marriage, and may be represented by particular fashion brands. A master-and-slave relationship was a strong one but primarily functional in purpose (and you thought we were talking about something else, you naughty reader) and often captured relationships we felt locked into, such as gym and utility contracts. These relationships may seem behaviorally very loyal on the surface, but the feelings of resentment felt by these consumers mean that they are very open to switching should an alternate present itself.

These relationship metaphors were also useful for understanding consumer reactions to perceived or real failures. At the time there was a strangely long-lived, but largely non-replicated idea of the 'service recovery paradox', whereby consumers suffering a wrong in their dealings with the brand would become more loyal to (and even an advocate for) the brand if the error was recovered or managed well. Likely taking inspiration from conspiracy theorists who argued that the massive failure of New Coke was intentional, some even wondered if we should deliberately trigger failures, in the belief the humiliation and return to long-held band truths would make consumers love the brand more (as a sidenote, this idea of the marketing fail conspiracy still continues, and since we live in a world defined by truthiness, might offer an aspiring brand consultant an opening as 'massive brand failure to rebirth' specialist). They argued service recovery would be easier and quicker where the relationship was strong because consumers would be more forgiving, whereas weaker relationships would lead to angrier outbursts.

Sounds all very sensible until it hit the reality of the marketplace. Turns out customers in the strongest brand relationships were the most aggrieved even if the infraction was objectively tiny. Those experiencing massive failures in weak relationships actually seemed comparatively chilled. Some examples should help (they usually do). One consumer discussed the decision by L'Oréal to remove one hand cream she liked. No biggie you'd think, right? Wrong, she was positively outraged and broke the relationship angrily. Another couple discussed how a bank worker gave away their financial information to a member of the public in a small rural town. Now if anything should get you outraged, this is it. Nope, they were so chilled one actually wanted to slap them out of it. What was going on?

Turns out the nature of the brand relationship could amplify anger in the first case, while in the second, it provided a buffer to it (Beverland et al. 2010). This qualitative insight is supported by extensive quantitative evidence and is called 'love-becomes-hate effect' (Grégoire et al. 2009). Turns out that L'Oréal with their promise of 'because you're worth it' had set themselves up for feelings of betrayal because they had effectively cheated on their customer. The bank, well they tend to be more functionally minded and the customer just wanted the situation fixed and services to continue. Customers in relationships that were less emotionally intense tended to be more forgiving. Similar examples affect brands like the utilitarian Toyota who had some unplanned acceleration issues in their vehicles in the United States. Yes, the problem hurt financially, but the brand soon rebounded in terms of consumer equity. As Fournier would say, be careful what you wish for, as relationship types come with separate sets of rules and expectations of behavior, with feelings of betrayal particularly hard to recover from, especially since offering economic compensation only makes the situation worse (try cheating on your partner and then offering them an expensive treat as compensation and see what happens).

Fournier's 2 × 2 matrix also enabled her to classify a range of relationships which could then be quantified and refined, then tracked in terms of their likely trajectory. A fling for example will be short-lived, passionate, and irrational, meaning that brands should try and milk these relationships for all they're worth while they are there. A spousal relationship though is more enduring, involves give-and-take and mutual understanding, and be viewed as more of an equal partnership. Understanding trajectories provides insights in terms of how relationships could be managed, while also identifying which relationships could be more valuable. Fournier's subsequent work also examined the potential connections between relationships to provide managers with insight into the possibilities and means to nudge consumers from a low- to high-value one.

What drove consumers to see their brands in particular ways? Their identity goals and the context of their lived experience. Understanding these two factors was the secret to understanding customer loyalty, understanding how to shift relationships (in favor of the brand), or why consumers may experience a sense of shock, and even pain, when their brand relationship partners do not respond in kind. For example, in promoting her work Fournier (2012) provides three collages that represent how three different consumers view the Starbucks brand. For one consumer, the collage reflects her busy life as a working mother where she has little time for herself and few escapes from the drudgery of work, motherhood, being a wife, and so on. For her, Starbucks is an indulgence each morning on the way to work, something that is solely for her. For a retired gentleman consumer, Starbucks represents a trip to what sociologists' call 'the third place' (after work and home), whereby he can escape all his children and grandchildren and be with friends his own age (a strategy that has frustrated coffee shop owners ever since, as consumers spend hours in store but purchase little). For the third consumer, the ability to afford Starbucks (after all, a brand deserves a premium), is indicative that she is making her way in the world, and that her hard work is paying off. Three different consumers, three different lives, three different brand relationships.

Fournier's work in many ways is much misunderstood by managers. Calls by former Saatchi & Saatchi CEO Kevin Roberts (2004) to turn brands into 'Lovemarks' fail to recognize that consumers may have perfectly valuable relationships with brands that nonetheless do not reach the emotional state of love. Moving consumers to more valuable relationships may make sense to a growth-driven brand manager but not fit within the goals and lifestyle of the consumer (in which case much CRM effort is wasted). And relationships can change in ways that have very little to do with the brand (getting a new job for example may result in changes in brand relationships), and it is therefore futile to talk about all the good times you have had.

What Fournier's research also showed is that behavioral loyalty tells you little about the why of brand consumption. A consumer in a relationship with a brand they view as an abusive partner may look like they're very loyal, but a lack of choice or particularly life circumstances may dictate necessity of use. If either of these situations change, what appears to be a heavily loyal consumer may run for their life. Likewise, once the mother in Fournier's famous Starbucks example sees her children off to school, manages to get a better paying job, or less likely, finds her husband willing to help out with his kids, then her relationship with the brand may change, in unpredictable ways. For Fournier, loyalty was dynamic, unpredictable, multi-faceted, and difficult to manage (as another one of her highly influential academic articles demonstrated; Fournier and Mick 1999).

Consumer Culture Theory (CCT) and brands

Consumer culture research has expanded our understanding of the role of brands in people's lives. Whereas psychological approaches tend to assume consumers have agency and act according to their preferences, consumer culture research identifies that consumers operate within structures that limit their agency. For example, examinations of taste and class identify that consumers from working-class backgrounds often choose overt ostentatious signs of luxury to reflect their taste (Holt 1998). Why? Often because they have been brought up in an environment where having more money represents success. However, those born into money have been brought up differently. With their ability to take economic wealth for granted, taste for these consumers reflects their cultural capital, or their ability to discuss, usually pretentiously, fine-grained nuances and details of less ostentatious brands. In practice, when working-class consumers try to fit in with upper-class consumers through consumption, they fail spectacularly and remain largely unaware that they are doing so.

These structures limit choice and can include gender and racial norms, age, location, plus many others. Mid-level structures can also form within brand communities that reflect communally-held expectations or can arise through institutionalized preferences that may lead to unintended discrimination or exclusion (such as the idealization of certain body types in fashion school training, often reinforced by mannequin sizes that have received little updating since the 1920s, leading to a lack of stylish plus-sized clothing).

One further difference from psychological approaches to branding is the unit of analysis. Psychological approaches to branding focus on the individual consumer and their decisions, whereas consumer culture research focuses on individuals, groups and even nations. Apart from brand communities for example, researchers have identified how brand managers may create imagined communities among nations. For example, Julien Cayla and Giana Eckhardt (2008) noted that during the FIFA World Cup hosted by Korea and Japan, brand managers created the concept of a 'New Asia' to provide the basis to launch new local brands or reposition existing ones to a global audience. This imagined community downplayed the enormous differences between a range of nations that had a long history of conflict in favor of a stylized set of shared myths, iconography, and brands.

Subsequent studies expanded on this further, shifting attention from opportunities for brands through formal events such as the FIFA World Cup to the ways consumers used brands to make sense of disruptions that often upended collective notions of identity. In contrast to the glamourous brands we often associate with particular nations as outsiders, insiders use mundane, everyday, downright average brands to heal a sense of collective loss. Former citizens of the German Democratic Republic (GDR) for example were instrumental in reviving simple brands of condiments as a means of countering the belief that everything in the GDR was inferior to the capitalist West (Brunk et al. 2018). The rise of Māori identity in New Zealand coupled with economic disruption saw local Pākehā (New Zealanders of European descent) feel they were suddenly citizens of nowhere. The same type of ubiquitous brands that cut across race and class lines played a prominent role in the co-creation of a new 'Kiwi' identity, offering a 'somewhere' for these disrupted citizens (Beverland et al. 2021).

Navigating this space is fraught with difficulty, however. The creation of Kiwi culture simply returned the dominant majority to their place of power, and arguably has not seen off the rise of populism that has undermined the ability to deal with collective challenges such as race relations, climate change, and wealth disparities. Local Austrian brands found themselves abandoned by long-time local loyalists when they started to adapt their offerings to the second generation of Turkish immigrants. Original locals (or *indigenes*) felt that such actions undermined Austrian traditions and represented a dilution of their culture (Luedicke 2015). Brand managers may feel unduly hurt when they are punished for being customer-focused, but such results underline Fournier's complex relational view of brands as carriers of meaning.

While this school of research remains small relative to the psychologically-informed majority, it is decidedly within academic marketing's mainstream and, given its discovery focus, provides newly-generated insights for the more experimentally minded to test. In 2005 this group of researchers was, unknowingly, branded as 'consumer culture theory'. Armed with a range of qualitative methods, they have now developed a whole host of theories and insights that sometimes complement, sometimes contradict models of brand building (such as Keller's), a point we make in our own brand textbook (please buy it), but generally always enriches our understanding of the consumers' lived experience of branding. Without these insights, we would have a more restricted view of brand building and would have struggled to keep pace with new practices such as person-brands, brand boycotts, brands and identity, and cultural branding.

Douglas Holt: branding's citizen artist

Just as Keller drew on an emerging stream of research on the psychology of brands to formulate his model of customer-based brand equity,

Douglas Holt, former L'Oréal Chair at Oxford, drew on these cultural insights to offer a radically different model of branding. Pioneering what is called the cultural model of branding, Holt (2004) undertook historical case analysis of what he called icon brands. Icons brands were not as dead as the term suggests; but were instead enduring mass-market brands that often cut across class, income, and racial divides within a nation. He covered such well-known brands as Nike, Harley Davidson, Budweiser, and Coke.

Holt noted that brands were carriers of culture and were successful not through an emphasis on abstract values that never changed (what is often termed 'positioning' and will be covered in the next chapter), but because they shifted with the times, switching from one meaning to the next to maintain their relevance. Holt argued that brands should be 'citizen artists', seeking to contribute cultural material as part of a broader social role that would help cement their relevance within people's lives.

There's more to Holt's model than one can cover here, although he has tended to have more success with advertising agencies (who have long practiced the art of reading cultural shifts to shape the relevance of brands) than by going direct to brand managers. Holt is often highly critical of psychological approaches to branding, or what he labels 'mindshare'. He believes that failure to understand consumers' needs for 'we-ness' means brands struggle to (1) change when needed, and (2) take advantage of disruptions to culture, and (3) leverage culture authentically.

Holt argues that mindshare models (i.e., customer-based brand equity) are too abstract and, much like more recent behavioral approaches (covered below), miss the simple reasons that lie behind most brand purchases. He argues that in an attempt to be scientific, branding has become 'sciency' which means science-like, but without the predictive power enjoyed by disciplines such as physics or biology (although possibly more than economics) (Holt and Cameron 2010). This desire to appear scientific means brand managers struggle to break out of an iron cage or what he calls a 'brand bureaucracy', whereby anything off-brand (e.g., off-target market, off-position, inconsistent with the brand's past communications) is filtered out of discussions. As a result, brand managers track consumers perceptions of relatively meaningless concepts, invest marketing resources into reinforcing those concepts in the minds of consumers, and never straying too far from the formula.

This brand bureaucracy reflects the same type of confirmation bias that fans of brands use to filter out negative information about their choices. Researchers call this a 'mental frame' or a 'thought world', whereby one's beliefs about the right way to view the world, or in branding, a problem, determines what information you focus on, what data you accept as valid, and what actions you undertake. The problem is these mental frames usually offer an incomplete answer to the problem (Holt is fully on board with mindshare when it comes to understanding brand extension, although a study on authentic extension by Spiggle et al. (2012) suggests culture can inform brand extension as well), and thereby limit your ability to fully understand the nature of reality. Of course, in a sense, Holt is a victim of his own bureaucracy, which leads him to overstate the value of peripheral insights (which may help with challenger brands but not mass brands) and the need for constant pivoting (long-term brand endurance has been demonstrated to involve reframing brand elements in ways relevant for the times).

practitioner voices

Branding theory and practice have always coexisted, often in an uneasy relationship. Giants such as Wally Olins (1978) have triggered sub-specialisms of academic branding research (e.g., corporate identity), while many of the key concepts of branding covered in the next chapter have their origins in practice. On the other hand, many of the academics covered so far spend (or have spent) much of their time in the field, often driving practice rather than simply capturing and organizing it. David Aaker for example has founded his own agency, Prophet, which has given far greater prominence to relevance in brand valuations, urging brands to be even more meaningful in the lives of consumers. Designers such as Marty Neumeier (2005) have developed wonderfully useful tools to help people think clearly about brands and strategy (one of which we cover in the next chapter). With zippy titles like *The Brand Flip* and *Zag*, Neumeier urges managers to always look for relevant points of difference and deliver on them effectively through every possible touchpoint as a means of standing out from the pack while playing to one's own strengths. An interaction designer by training, he highlights the potential sensory significance of even the smallest touchpoint elements in the consumer's brand experience.

Finally, high-profile award-winning industry journalists such as Helen Edwards and Mark Ritson (who gives celebrity chef and media personality Gordon Ramsay a run for his money in the use of profanities) help translate academic ideas into practice. Edwards is an early pioneer on the notion of purpose with her work on 'passion brands', which very much channeled a mix of psychological and cultural insights and laid them over classic frameworks for creating brand value. Edwards (2018) has also been at the forefront of pushing back against claims that customers have little emotional investment in brands, drawing on experimental studies that examine the potential for brand love for example (in her words, consumers might not love brands in the sense you love your partner or your own reflection, but there is something akin to heightened emotion in some brand relationships). Ritson is an ex-academic (and a successful one at that), and blends up-to-date practice and data, with what he argues are tried-and-true principles of branding. In this sense he is more of a traditionalist, urging caution in embracing technological and ideological fads, and together with Edwards, is running an online mini-MBA in branding that benefits from their extensive reputations.

Claims by the likes of Douglas Holt that brand management is sciency are deserved, if not completely fair. Experienced practitioners draw on substantive amounts of data, from quantitative tracking to focus group and ethnographic (and now, online, netnographic) research. Although they may lament their lack of power (don't we all?), organizations arguably take branding more seriously than ever, and therefore demand greater accountability for how their key asset(s) is managed. This has seen a greater emphasis on marketing effectiveness, with brand managers becoming far more strategic in their approach. Although they're playing catch-up on the financial impact of brand investments, the days of soft measures such as awareness and satisfaction being enough are over (although social media marketers are often still relentlessly parodied in titles such as Marketing Week as attributing 'likes' to financial success).

The Marketing Effectiveness Awards, a.k.a. the *Effies*, require contestants to connect the context of their actions with research-driven insights, strategic and tactical responses, and demonstrable outcomes. One of the authors of this book is a judge on these panels and can confirm just how much unanimity exists between creatives, strategists, academics, and thought leaders on the need to have a clear strategic goal and links between it and research insights, subsequent creative campaign, and financial outcomes. Those with more creative roles on award panels are often the most skeptical about unsupported claims (although this could be simply jealousy that they didn't think of the entrant's idea themselves).

This emphasis on effectiveness has been a long time coming and has had to deal with claims that it stifles creativity (the opposite is true) and leads to short-termism. The latter claim is also unfounded – as Binet and Field (2013) demonstrate in their analysis of Effie Award winners, one needs to connect the short (up to six months) and long term (a year). The short-term impact is necessary to move the consumer up the CBBE pyramid (or in modern parlance, create mental availability) by creating the basis for the initial purchase that helps shape the consumer's knowledge of the brand through experience. Combined, these effects help shape long-term brand image, and build loyalty. Practitioners are not immune from fads and fashions, and indeed may be forced by short-term risk averse managers to place bets on new technologies and innovations such as aligning with social causes or investing in storytelling. However, greater emphasis on effectiveness and return on investment (which comes with the claim that brands are assets) quickly weeds out those that fail to deliver (although rarely generates the reflexivity necessary to cease the fad cycle, especially those of the technological variety).

Ehrenberg-Bass: brand science from a land down under

Some go even further, arguing for a science of branding, seeking to develop immutable laws, or empirical generalizations. Long known for their contrarian, and dare we say, curmudgeonly demeanor at marketing conferences, Byron Sharp and his team of branded colleagues (clones who were often dubbed the Byronites and Byronettes in less politically correct times) from the University of South Australia (rebranded as Adelaide University in 2023) delighted in telling every other marketing scientist that they were wrong. Whereas most academics are motivated by the novelty of their contribution (you won't get published in the top journals without one, which in itself creates an industry based on new things), Sharp and his colleagues took a more unfashionable route, arguing that only through replication could you build up empirical generalizations (they even started their own journal dedicated to just that – alas, it never really caught on). Constantly demanding that academics move beyond interesting one-off studies or war stories to provide law-like generalizations, they leveraged their access to large amount of purchase data from large fast moving consumer goods brands. The result was to question one of the core assumptions of brand practice, that appealing to loyalists was the best way to grow brand value.

Acting as the smartest person in the room rarely wins friends, and in the academic realm, the South Australia crew, eventually named the Ehrenberg–Bass Institute after two famous marketing scientists who found patterns in brand purchase and began modeling them in the early 1970s, were initially regarded with a degree of derision. While the likes of Keller (1993) had incorporated some of Andrew Ehrenberg's pioneering work into his original model, it was practitioners, particularly those outside of the United States, that really took Sharp and his colleagues' insights to heart.

The Ehrenberg–Bass work focuses heavily on tracking behavior. Like Keller, they argue brands need to build knowledge structures (which they label mental availability) in the minds of consumers, but where they differ is in the depth of that knowledge. Whereas Keller is open to the consumer being akin to a sponge, joyfully soaking up more and more brand knowledge (deeper knowledge structures leads to stronger relationships thereby more loyalty), Sharp views the consumer more like a bored student, wanting to know just what is in the exam, and preferably via a short video. They argue that consumers see little difference between brands and really want marketers just to tell them what makes their brand special, or in their parlance, distinctive (which should not be confused with difference, and never ever ever with uniqueness).

The root of what is now one of the most influential approaches to brand management in practice began in the early 1990s at the University of South Australia in Adelaide. The marketing team there gained access to large amounts of sales data from the many global FMCG brands that were headquartered in the city. Large amounts of data may sound like manna from heaven for academics, but it brings with it some challenges. The biggest one is how to analyze it effectively. Remember in the 1990s, many of the statistical programs we have now were only in their infancy, so managing very large sets of data was cumbersome and required a substantial amount of computing power. More importantly, this challenge required a framework to structure all these data. Enter the works of Frank Bass who had pioneered a model of diffusion of innovations that allowed for greater predictability of new product success, and more critically, of Andrew Ehrenberg, a statistician who believed one could apply natural science principles to the social sciences, in particular marketing.

Ehrenberg's most significant contribution to the field of marketing is his Dirichlet Model of buyer behavior which models brand purchases across a range of different categories and contexts (Goodhardt et al. 1984). Described by Sharp (2010, p. 217) as 'one of marketing's few true scientific theories', Ehrenberg's work was driven by a number of principles including the need for simplicity and economy of scope (of variables and factors taken into account), the need for substantive replication of any simple model and the absence of bias in prediction. With these principles in mind, Ehrenberg and some colleagues uncovered a range of law-like empirical generalizations, the most famous of which include double jeopardy (which identifies a relationship between market share, number of brand buyers, and their loyalty, suggesting that larger brands gain a double benefit from their size), natural monopoly (brands with more market share attract a greater proportion of light category buyers (Sharp 2010), and the duplication of purpose law (which basically holds that customers typically buy from a small number of a brands in a category, i.e., they are split-loyal rather than fanatics).

Through sustained replications across a whole range of categories, from what we label as low involvement (i.e., they don't trigger much emotional depth) FMCG's to more high involvement (i.e., categories that may generate great interest), Sharp, along with Ehrenberg and many others perfected these laws and added a range of others, arguing that it was behavior *per se* that was the best predictor of brand choice, rather than any stated attitudes or intentions (in fact one of their laws argues that attitudes and intentions are simply outcomes of behavior). Armed with data, Sharp, Ehrenberg and others challenged an emerging status quo regarding the value of loyalty, the existence of niche brands with special management principles, and that brands are built slowly, over many years (among other insights).

These insights were collected in Byron Sharp's massively influential book *How Brands Grow*, which was published in 2010. To Sharp's surprise, *How Brands Grow*, became a best seller, shifting over 50,000 copies (which really annoys those of us who claim best seller status by selling our 3,000-print run, although Sharp would probably advise us not to appeal to a narrow niche). It's fair to say the book gained more traction in Australasia and the United Kingdom than within the United States, where dedication to loyalists remains the order of the day. A Part Two followed, and the Ehrenberg–Bass team continues to publish insights that all too often are received uncritically or rejected too easily by fans and haters respectively. Either way, Ehrenberg–Bass have a sway and influence over parts of the marketing profession that others can only dream of (and probably an expense account that would make our eyes water).

Sharp and his team have built something akin to a cult of followers around them, both within academia and more widely, among practitioners. This is rather ironic given their love of empirical generalizations and scientific marketing framing, but one cannot control the actions of followers. This is a shame as it tends to feed into an equally strong rejection of their work by those who confuse the tone of the message and blind obedience of their fan club with the actual insights provided. Strangely, those on the more creative side of the industry are the harshest critics, even though Sharp argues strongly for the power of creative, going so far as to state that the insights of the group require better and more creativity, albeit within a framework of effectiveness (which is perhaps why some creatives, focused on winning Cannes Lions, get their knickers in a twist). At the same time, the work is not without limitations, including assumptions around static markets and claims of unoriginality.

That said, terms such as mental availability (which is simply a reframing of Keller's focus on building brand knowledge), brand assets (covered later), penetration and reach (both of which are measures of share and usage, and critical measures for any brand manager) have entered mainstream practitioner marketing discourse and it is important to understand them. The focus of Ehrenberg–Bass is obvious (growing brands), and it is probably this focus that ensures their success. Those old enough to remember the dot-com boom of the late 1990s will remember all the pitches by tech bro wannabes that focused on winning just one per cent of the one per cent of the total market. It sounded impressive if one looked at the raw numbers, but of course no financier and certainly no shareholder is interested in numbers that small. Likewise, claims that different categories are exempt from some of Sharp's laws have been shown to be questionable and perhaps explain why brand managers or CEOs from FMCG groups such as Unilever can successfully manage luxury groups and vice versa.

Strangely, the book had far less impact on academics. Part of this came down to the fact that we had largely been here before. Perhaps the authoritative tone of the book, with its announcement of laws and denunciation of core thinkers was off-putting to academics who tended to be skeptical of those claiming that they'd discovered the truth. For many years the group also provided little theorization for their results. They could identify what was happening, but not why. With an emphasis on the predictive power of behavior (rather than intentions), prior to *How Brands Grow*, they often characterized the consumer as a 'black box', in so far as it wasn't important to know why something occurred, as long as one could accurately predict what would occur. This of course commits the cardinal academic sin of poor or no theorization and will never get you published in the world's best journals.

Sharp refuses to drink the loyalty Kool-Aid and is extremely dismissive of the suggestion that consumers find deeper meanings in brands. Instead, he argues (or would say 'irrefutably demonstrates') that to grow brands (and if you're a publicly traded company, you have no alternative) appealing to lighter, less loyal, or indeed not-yet-loyal consumers is far more critical than worrying about loyalists. Loyal consumers for Sharp and his team were a fickle lot (perhaps for all the reasons people like Fournier found) and were easily wooed by alternative brands (which weren't much different anyway), switching away within a year. Appealing to them alone not only ignored too much of the market, but was likely to make large brands small, in reasonably quick time. Appealing to those small groups of true loyalists who hung around in communities was even more wasteful, since they preferred brands to remain very true to their roots. As postmodern marketer Stephen Brown

(2016) cautions, perhaps customers, far from being right, are just right wing, stuck-in-the-mud conservatives.

chapter summary

One of our supervisors once ended his presentation on trends and challenges for industry with a joke that, like all academics, he had provided no clear answers but hopefully some insights. There is of course truth to this, but we can also see the interplay between real world challenges, academic research and practice have defined brand management for at least a century. All the leading writers covered above engage with industry, often extensively, or work within industry settings to provide theoretical and practical breakthroughs such as brand communities. Throughout, we see three main drivers of branding knowledge:

1. Defining the nature and scope of branding: Over time, we have moved from proto brands with their emphasis on traceability through to a focus on building identity, image, and distinctiveness. These insights have been driven by different approaches to consumer motivation.
2. The value of loyalty: From something that was largely viewed through the lens of trust, to goodwill that was treated as an accounting liability, to an overemphasis on retention vs. acquisition and back again, loyalty lies at the heart of branding, and by extension, brand valuation.
3. The value of brands to firms: Much of the modern focus on understanding brands has been driven by a recognition that one can compete symbolically rather than just through price competitiveness or breakthrough innovations. The concern with how one could financially value a brand way above marketplace expectations led to an emphasis on how these assets could be managed for growth and has led researchers from a range of backgrounds to provide usable insights for practitioners.

Despite the rough and tumble of much of this debate, the interdisciplinary nature of brand research and practice and the links between industry, consumers, academia, and other stakeholders are admirable. While an emphasis on simple laws may deny the richness of consumers' brand experience, searching for them is worthwhile, and there is often far more crossover in terms of implications than their adherents would care to admit. With a very brief look at key thought leaders out of the way, let's turn to some core constructs and practices in brand management that are essential to know.

4
How to Speak Like a Branding Pro

We will never miss an opportunity to sell our textbook; so once again, we must seek to differentiate this guide from a more comprehensive examination of brand management. However, in an age where performativity is king and anyone armed with some TikTok knowledge can make it as a person-brand social media influencer, this section aims to arm you with some of the core concepts of brand management that will let you talk about branding like a pro. Joking aside, understanding some of the basics are critical for any manager, given the power of branding as a tool for value creation. Knowing some of this might also force your marketing team to be a bit more on edge and up their game, which is tragically more necessary than you would think.

how much is that doggie in the window? brand equity and all that

What is a brand worth to you? Would you pay extra for it? Would you line up overnight to get the latest drop? Would you take a cut in salary to work for a brand? Or demand a higher salary to work for another? What could we ask for the brand if we were putting it up for sale? These rather instrumental questions all concern one of the more contested issues in brand management, brand equity.

Why contested? Before answering that we need to define what we mean by equity. Equity in branding largely refers to a differential effect of the brand on something or someone. For marketers that effect might be the impact of the brand on the effectiveness of your marketing. Swifties (fans of pop superstar Taylor Swift) camping out overnight in the cold for a Record Store Day release (that they may not even have the means to listen to) are doing so because the brand has an impact on the product (a new album, or more likely, a shameless cash-in via a repackaged old one). If consumers notice your advertising, or a business buyer opens the door for your salespeople, it is because the brand is making an important difference (or creating 'pull' as we say). We call this customer-based brand equity, and it simply refers to the effect the brand has on behavior.

There are other ways of thinking about brand equity, but the logic of a differential effect does not change. So in answer to whether you'd make a salary sacrifice or demand a better offer to work for a particular brand, we called this employer brand equity, or the difference the brand makes on employees (present and future). This is important because attracting and keeping talent is essential in economies driven by services and creativity (including products and business-to-business). This area is perhaps where the issue of brand purpose, covered in the next chapter, does matter, as employees do want to work for employers they are proud of and who embody their ethics.

We may also talk about channel equity, which is one of the most important and neglected aspects of the brand as an asset. Put simply, will your channel partners feature the brand in the best shelf space, give it prominence on their landing page, encourage their staff to promote it, and so on. You could easily extend this to influencer equity as a form of channel, whereby person-brands use and promote your brand because they genuinely like it, or discount their rates (influencers have to eat too) because your brand enhances theirs (a similar effect can occur in business services where top advertising agencies, for example, may lower their initial rates because they want your prestigious brand on their books). Most large channels like strong brands, largely because they bring consumers to them and will want to work more closely with them in a strategic partnership. Should you be tempted to exploit this imagined power by throwing your weight around with channel partners, don't be surprised if they use their real market power to dramatically reduce your brand's equity (channel partners do not view brand relationships in emotional terms, unless they think of you using language that we cannot possibly use in a study guide with a G-rating).

The difference the brand makes on the balance sheet of the firm is far more contentious, with many questioning whether you can really measure this accurately. The criticism is compounded by the inability of major brand valuation agencies to agree, or even come close to agreeing, on rankings and valuations. While some are tempted to say, 'you can only ever know what the brand is worth when you sell it', this suggests that the buyer is making an objective valuation, when all they are doing is making a bet. From failed brand mergers to written-off acquisitions, buyers often get it wrong, while those who suggest too much was paid, such as much of the media when Bernard Arnault purchased Louis Vuitton, are often spectacularly wrong.

Does all this matter, and if so, how are these values calculated? For marketers, such valuations might provide bragging rights, even power (but don't count on it), but an increase in valuation probably matters more for the CEOs of publicly listed companies or those start-ups hoping to attract investors. Why? Most of a firm's value lies in intangibles and the brand is arguably one of the biggest intangible assets of all. Those too reliant on tangible assets can be ripe for takeover or even being split up and sold off. This emphasis on intangibles is why clients pushed the management consultancy company Interbrand to develop a system to measure whether their brand advice was sound.

Interbrand every year compile a top 100 list (unassumingly named 'The Best Global Brands') of the most valuable brands, as measured by them. How do they rank each? This is largely kept secret, but in a clever bit of sciency politics, was claimed to be as good as any other metric in a series of articles written in some of the less scrupulous academic marketing journals in the late 1980s (Power 1992). We say politics, because the articles were largely identical, but written by different groups of Interbrand authors, and submitted to journals that at the time had little, if any, peer review (Penrose and Moorhouse 1989). However, the audience for this work was not aware of the subtle snobbery academics deploy to judge journals, and hence the Interbrand method (which has subsequently changed a few times) was given market legitimacy. Although the first mover, Interbrand now have several competitors, all with slightly different methods and approaches, which often given rise to radically different results.

The process of valuation per se is not particularly controversial – basically you try and dissociate the impact of the brand from other activities within a particular geographic market, multiply it by the strength of the customer relationship with the brand, and moderate it for risk and growth potential in the segment. Sounds simple, but the first, as financially minded marketers such as Patrick Barwise (1993) from the London Business School argued, was impossible. The second is contentious, requires actual consumer data (as opposed to assessments made from desk research), and as we've heard, may be much less valuable or powerful than thought, while the last bit is relatively easier. Mark Ritson has long challenged Interbrand on this issue, suggesting that assessments of brand strengths by newly minted graduates in New York isn't that accurate (he also points out that even with libel laws that favor plaintiffs in the United Kingdom, he has never been sued by the consulting company, although he could just be lying).

In a world where one is bombarded with lists suggestive of brand equity, from questionable measures of your brand's 'coolness' to LinkedIn polls of most desired brands to work for, the best cities to live in, and so on, through to those evaluating your brand's power and relevance, it is difficult to avoid cherry picking those rankings that make you look good (i.e., confirmation bias). Who after all doesn't want to be a 'cool brand'? (Since they tend to be based on votes by the general public modified by a group of experts, these measures are rarely useful as a management tool, although they might give you an opportunity to exploit the moment).

Perhaps focusing on the power of the brand closer to home is more useful. Accurately pricing a brand is probably a futile exercise, but measuring the impact of a brand remains worthwhile. Although financial experts may disagree with the term, brands are identified as assets (as opposed to a brand's assets, see below), which means they require investment and management. Longitudinal studies that identify the pricing premium enjoyed by brands across shifting economic cycles provide the basis for return-on-investment decisions (and take away any excuse by less financially minded marketers that one cannot measure the value of brand-driven marketing activity).

Being honest about the fleeting strength of the consumer relationship underpinning brand valuation actually provides an empirical basis for both sustained investment and also for keeping the brand fresh through new 'activations', including an investment in the core activities that underpin a brand's value (such as product, service, ease of availability and use, identity value, and so on). Finally, recognizing that investing in brand equity may have other organizational benefits, often not customer focused, is one way of building greater support for brand marketing within the firm (think about the benefits to human resources of strong employer brand equity, for example).

who are you? the identity issue

Possibly the core consideration of any brand development program concerns issues of identity. Often labelled positioning, or brand position, this refers to the essential DNA that will define the brand (and its supporting marketing programs) for years to come. It is underpinned by research and also drives all subsequent marketing and non-marketing activities (if you think of branding as an onion as some consultants like to do, the brand position is the core of the onion). Although the idea that a brand will aim to own a space in the mind of the target consumer is relatively simple, and even uncontroversial, achieving this is remarkably difficult in practice, not the least due to groupthink and a lack of discipline over time. More recently, critics of different persuasions have started to question its usefulness, while never quite being able to escape its orbit.

The origin of the idea has many different sources. A *Harvard Business Review* article in 1959 written by academic Sid Levy called 'Symbols for Sale' argued that brand identity should shift from clearly denoting a benefit, usually related to functional performance, to connoting more abstract ideals, that were more emotional, and identity-driven. Management response to the article was positive, largely because it reflected a wider shift in advertising for brands at the time. Although it's common to view this period as one where consumers were passive receivers of brand meaning, this belies the immense amount of effort major agencies such as Ogilvy and JWT undertook to capture the zeitgeist of the times and understand changes in subsequent behavior. And, for many brands, identity was created or shaped by advertising, and as such was seen more as a goal to work toward, or realize, than the strategic compass that became more typical from the 1990s onwards.

Other influences on this idea came in the form of Ries and Trout's best-selling *Positioning: The Battle for your Mind* (1981), which has enjoyed several follow-ups and anniversary editions. Although their claim for originating the idea of position is perhaps overstated, Ries and Trout's ideas have nonetheless had a significant impact on practice and were even incorporated into academic models of brand management. As the title indicates, brand managers should aim to own some mental real estate with their target consumers. Writing at a time when brands were proliferating and economic downturn was driving influential practitioners to muse on the crisis in branding (which was largely a debate about whether cheap own-label or private-label retailer brands would displace manufacturer brands as consumers became more economically rational), Ries and Trout argued that having a very clear positioning relative to consumer needs and competitor offerings was essential to cut through the clutter and survive.

Wally Olins, co-founder of the London-based Wolff Olins branding agency, suggested in 1978 that organizations could have a personality, giving birth to the corporate branding field that would define his firm's point of difference for decades and also lead practitioners to emphasize consistency of look, tone, and feel throughout every aspect of what later on became known as the 'consumer journey' (which encompasses all the ways the consumer interacts with the brand before, during, and after purchase).

In contrast to Ries and Trout, Olins' clients were primarily in the service sector that was burgeoning in post-industrial UK. If marketers wanted consumers to form a clear view of their providers, then every aspect of the encounter had to speak with the same voice, which led to a greater focus not just on advertising, but also on staff training and all forms of direct and indirect communications design (from letterheads to lanyards and uniforms through to architecture). This gave rise to an interest in internal branding, to ensure staff were aligned with the desired brand identity, and also to engaging other stakeholders for the same reason. Today, marketers are therefore encouraged to examine gaps between their desired identity, their culture, and how external stakeholders view the brand. Olins' work to change British Petroleum to 'Beyond Petroleum' in the 1990s stands as an example of what happens when these gaps remain unaddressed, with the program often seen as an exemplar of what would become known as greenwashing.

Budding brand managers now spend time and substantial sums of money on defining a brand's position or identity. However, this is where things get tricky. While the idea is simple in theory, in practice, getting agreement on what will be the unchanging idea that defines the brand or corporation is fraught with difficulty, and often politics. Mark Ritson, the foul-mouthed award-winning journalist and educator on all things branding, often runs an exercise called 'The Graveyard of Shit' in his classes. The exercise involves using a Harvard Business School case (what else?) to help MBA students understand how to build a brand's position and then apply that to make effective tactical marketing decisions, by asking students to identify ideas that could define the brand.

What goes into the aforementioned graveyard? The comforting words we can all agree on, including such commonly used ideas as 'different', 'innovative', 'trust', 'excellence', and so on. In branding terms, these ideas have no workable opposites, and are seen as vanilla (another metaphor Ritson deploys) – a flavor no one hates, but few, outside of dessert chefs, get excited about. The best brands, or at least those marketers all mythologize, are tightly defined and are not made to appeal to everyone, and they certainly embody an identity that has a workable opposite. For example, HSBC was built around the idea of 'considerate', which reflected the cultural diversity of the global banking group. This gave rise to the idea of 'the world's local bank', that was so successful as a brand appeal (until internal politics led to it being dropped in favor of claims such as 'tomorrow is another day') within an immensely competitive global landscape in which large banking groups carved out different identities offering essentially the same services.

Historically of course such exercises were unnecessary – with only little competition, entrepreneurs armed with new breakthrough products succeeded because they appealed to a mass market through investments in advertising that highlighted obvious benefits, sharp pricing, and widespread distribution. Today however, one must define one's brand before doing any of those things. So how?

An array of tools exists, some of which are complex, others too simple. Practitioners often love ball-sport metaphors like the sweet spot (perhaps they all play too much golf) to describe the ultimate goal of positioning exercises. This sweet spot usually involves trying to find a guiding idea that is relevant to one's target user, different from competitors, and deliverable in terms of your available resources.

Marty Neumeier offers a different take on this, asking aspiring brand marketers to write their brand obituaries (which is maybe not the most cheerful way to start building a brand). He urges wannabe brand managers to place themselves 20 years in the future and imagine that their brand has died. What was it admired for? Who admired it enough to attend the funeral? What difference did it make? These questions or variants on them seem to sit at the heart of many tools offered by experts. In practice these questions may seem remarkably simple, but they demand a discipline that many managers struggle with.

While the idea of positioning remained unchallenged for years, more recently questions have been asked about its value. Ideally the brand's position should remain unchanged, while changes in the marketing program help keep it fresh. This is a consistency–relevance challenge that will be explored in the next chapter, and it largely refers to never changing the brand's DNA, but always changing the products and services, spokespeople, designs, events, and so on to keep the brand relevant for the times.

Douglas Holt, originator of the cultural branding approach, argues that this claim fails the test of history. Many of the brands celebrated for never changing have in fact always changed. Budweiser, for example, was once a beer served to the middle-class man by his adoring wife on returning home from a hard day's work. Later, it was a reward for hardworking blue-collar men. Then it became something for lads to bond over, largely through making silly noises, much to bemusement of their female partners. Holt argues that brands must be prepared to throw out their positions in the face of large-scale cultural shifts that may render cherished brand ideals irrelevant. This makes sense, although Holt's own analysis also suggests that brands such as Budweiser have remained committed to the idea of a beer for men but have simply shifted their target consumer and communications to reflect shifts in the experience of masculinity over time.

Holt's other view is that positions are often far too abstract and thus easy to copy. Such abstract positions are often hard for marketing teams to interpret and work with, and do not reflect the prosaic connections consumers have with brands (which is why tools like the much maligned and abused consumer persona have become popular). Unexpectedly, those drawing on a behavioral tradition (such as the Ehrenberg–Bass

Institute) agree, suggesting that consumers see relatively little difference between brands and make choices based on perceived distinctiveness and availability. Although these authors diverge on the implications of this (Holt argues for brands to offer simple solutions to confused consumers, Ehrenberg–Bass calls for brands to stand out and to remind consumers what they do they do really well), they may both agree that complicated brand identity statements, replete with prisms and other geometric shapes, are unnecessary, pretentious, expensive, and potentially a barrier to relevance.

Undoubtedly brands need to stand for something, something that is relevant at least to customers, and that is a reference point for subsequent communications (what brand marketers call 'reinforcement'), but the nature of that ideal, and whether it should be set in stone, remain points of contention.

difference, distinction, uniqueness, and parity: what's the difference?

A brand should be different, or should it? Many years ago, one of us had the privilege of consulting to a large Australia paint retail brand. The CEO was a fun guy and passionate about retail. He loved to regale us with stories about the industry, in particular the way in which sales reps from different paint brands would try and find a point of difference in a product category where color choices were shared by all competitors and ingredients largely determined by law. Paint production was a mass manufacturing game, so competitors quickly copied each other, with benefits in relation to durability, ability to withstand the harsh Australian climate, sustainability, price, ease of use, and so on quickly becoming what we call points of parity (we will return to this below).

This led to absurd claims of difference including (and we wish we remembered the manufactured scientific term for this) the fact that only one paint had what was called a 'raindrop effect', which meant their paint was made so that raindrops would flow down the surface in an orderly fashion. Aussies are famous for their bullshit detectors and certainly we all smelled a rat. Who would really care? What did matter was that the industry was notoriously bad in how they treated the most important repeat, high-spend customer of the time – women. We decided to ignore the raindrops and focused most of our energies on training, in-store design, education, and communications, capturing share in the process.

This example captures a controversy over what should be non-controversial. For a long time, an emphasis on difference was taken for granted, a shibboleth (which is a fancy word for long standing principle) of brand practice. Some even went further arguing brands should be unique or have that essential unique selling point or USP. However, some have argued this has led brand managers to seek difference for difference's sake, such as the aforementioned raindrop effect, and that uniqueness ends up taking you away from a focus on consumer needs. More recently, distinction has entered the lexicon of brand managers, which on the face of it seems to be a meaningless distinction to differentiation, although nothing could be farther from the truth (at least according to its adherents).

The ideas of uniqueness and the USP didn't start out with the aim of disciplining unruly raindrops. Coming out of the practice of product innovation, sales, and supportive communications, the focus on relative difference was something that helped drive adoption of new things, especially when technological breakthroughs were meaningful. Relative difference in this sense usually meant noticeable, substantial, and valued (technical definitions that seem to have got lost). A focus on a USP in these domains often meant something important to consumers (and was usually tested carefully). These USP's enabled salespeople to cut to the chase with buyers and creatives to design advertisements that stood out or cut through the competitive clutter. However, an USP is hard to achieve and sustain in markets where differences tend to be symbolic and attributes are easily copied through software updates, fast fashion practices, and the recently common practice of copying competitors and sorting out compensation through legal means later (as tech bros are fond of saying 'it's better to ask for forgiveness than permission' although the courts are not so minded to abide by this). It also leads to function creep, or the never-ending search for performance advantages, which take brands further away from consumer needs and require deep pockets of resources and the capabilities (such as innovation and speed to market) that only large firms enjoy. The end of the line is of course the aforementioned raindrop effect.

With even meaningful USPs being temporary, these one-time points of difference (POD) quickly become what we call a point of parity. Points of parity (POP) can be understood in the old notion of the hygiene effect in organizational behavior – their absence may annoy customers, but their presence is not going to motivate admiration and purchase (Keller et al. 2002). POP are useful for ensuring one keeps up with competitors and are often the first thing you check the absence of when trying to revive a brand that has lost share. You may think that this would temper the search for unique points of difference (the same as USPs), but it's a hard idea to drop. With most understanding that functional uniqueness can be easily copied, some have argued that brands need to be emotionally different. But as Douglas Holt rightly notes, this is even worse as it replaces functional creep (which might at least be something you can protect) with emotional creep. Since emotions can rarely be trademarked, they can be even more easily copied and lead to a certain conversion among communications and messaging.

In 1998, US academics Joseph Pine and James Gilmore proposed that it was now the age of the experience economy (since people are sensory beings they were perhaps either late to the party or over-egging their claims). The logic was with most brands delivering the same functional benefits at similar price points, and also able to match one another on promises of love and desire, economies now needed to move to providing experiences. Two outcomes resulted from this – a huge investment in flagship experiential retail stores that were to embody the very essence of the brand and an emphasis on design. Shoe giant Nike, for example, built Nike Towns, which enabled customers to try out their products on in-store basketball courts (Bedbury 2002). Luxury stores bought up real estate in the most desirable neighborhoods and built museums or cathedrals to the brand, becoming destination shops in their own right, inviting the public to come and watch live concerts and poetry readings inside.

The idea is that if we experienced the brand at a perceptual, sensory level, it would get so under our skin that we would find it impossible to resist. The problem as that this strategy was expensive. Consumers may have been wowed by a destination store on first visit but quickly grew familiar with it, and then bored. Nike may have argued that the purpose of their towns was not to sell shoes, but to provide a full brand experience, but it was only the first part of that sentence that worked. In 2002, we visited Ralph Lauren's flagship Chicago store. It certainly made you feel as though you were inside F. Scott Fitzgerald's Ivy League influenced novel *The Great Gatsby*, but the costs of each fit-out were enormous, running into tens of millions each quarter, and requiring the store to be shut for a week, all of which resulted in further costs (and this was replicated across the globe). While many bet that consumers would not buy luxury online, it soon became clear that consumers were more than happy to, placing further strain on an expensive real-world experiential model (elements of the brand experience can be replicated online effectively).

Designers also seized the moment. Armed with swathes of Post-it Notes (whether they were 3M or another brand was neither here nor there), minimalist-designed glasses, and black clothing, these not-to-be-questioned artists tried to sell managers the merits of what became known as design thinking (which in reality is simply a form of problem-solving). Design certainly did seem to be critical to brands. No better example of this was the unexpected revitalization and eventual dominance of written-off technology pioneer Apple. Steve Jobs' return to the firm he co-founded was accompanied by British maestro, designer Johnny Ive. The intuitive nature of their breakthrough 'i' products disrupted leaders, confounded critics, and amazed consumers. Although design certainly was important (particularly when it was focused on enhancing the user experience), those poor executives forced to sit through endless sessions with method cards and Post-its quickly tired of design thinking. By 2011, design thinking was labelled 'dead' by Fast Company's Bruce Nussbaum (who was once one of its greatest proponents), and user experience increasingly became difficult to distinguish across brands. Apparently design thinking is still dead, or deader than dead, which you would think would negate the need for new articles on it.

So what's next? Whereas marketers are always swayed by snake oil salespeople from the tech industry, academics had started questioning the value of difference or uniqueness. The questions are really whether consumers see brands as different and whether that difference is meaningful. Cultural branders argued that difference had to be relevant, albeit only insofar as its relevance meant providing consumers with ways to repair broken cultural connections. Ehrenberg–Bass advocates provided data demonstrating that consumers rarely saw much difference between brands anyway, so why bother. But each had a slightly different view on how to proceed. Douglas Holt argued that a brand must be meaningfully different at a cultural level, or that it should speak to the zeitgeist of the times. If that changed, then the brand should similarly change, and if necessary, radically.

The Ehrenberg–Bass folks took another path. Not being particularly cultured (as in minded toward culturally informed research – we know you were thinking we were making implied judgments about Australians, which the first author as a naturalized Aussie would never do), they argued that brands should not strive for difference (and certainly never uniqueness), but distinctiveness. What is brand distinctiveness? Turns out it is defined as meaningfully different (as opposed to just different). This may seem like a semantic sleight of hand, and as with many Ehrenberg–Bass concepts, they are just a repackaging of what we know, but have often forgotten. Distinctiveness requires brand managers to really understand the value that their brands have delivered to customers over time. These benefits may not be different from those of other brands, but the brand owning them may have simply given greater emphasis to these benefits than others, or they may have been particularly good at delivering them. Furthermore, their managers may not have gotten distracted by searching for raindrop effects that meant nothing to consumers seeking solutions to problems.

Take the ABBA of the automotive world, Volvo. Before we even asked the question of the brand's distinctiveness you probably thought 'safety' right? Go on, you know you did. If you don't know cars, and neither of us are car people, we've run this experiment for years, across numerous classes around the world. The answer is always the same, Volvo is safe. Now, no car brand can be unsafe. There are laws against it, especially if one wants to sell in big markets like the United States. Cars, full of the most put-upon minority group, the crash test dummy, are literally destroyed by American safety regulators. All brands on the market are therefore safe, but only one embodies this as a point of distinctiveness, Volvo. Other brands stand for other things, many of which are hardly different or unique – Mercedes is status, BMW is the driving experience, Fiat is innovative use of space, Ford is utilitarian, Toyota is value-for-money, and Morgan is heritage. Each has spent years telling consumers what makes it distinctive. Each has ensured every bit of marketing messaging has stayed ruthlessly on point. And it worked, we got the message. This is why it is notoriously hard to start a new automotive brand or revive a tired old one.

Whereas cultural branders argue for radical change when the need arises, prophets of distinctiveness argue for something a bit trickier – that the brand must always be renewed (largely because loyalty is transient) but done so in a way that reminds consumers of what they know about the brand's distinctiveness. Why? Well, they also believe in mental availability, so radical change would conflict with what consumers, be they heavy or light users, already know about the brand. Secondly, although heavy buyers use drops off over time they still buy the brand, while newness is necessary to give lighter users or non-users a reason to try. There's a bit more than this, but nonetheless, change and stability are two things that are central to brand equity, the former building brand heritage or what we label as character, and the later as brand power or what we call improvisation (see how the desire for difference is not always a bad thing – even we're at it!). Basically your character builds your identity, your improvisation or power gives it is forward momentum or relevance.

We will cover the tension between stability and change in the last chapter, but for now an example will suffice. It will however involve one of the most dreadful teen romance series in history, responsible for revitalizing a genre that true to form, never seems to die: vampires.

When Stephanie Meyer's blockbuster *Twilight* series was turned into an equally massive film franchise (known as a serial brand in cultural brand circles), Volvo realized it had an opportunity to make its point of distinction relevant to a new audience, without losing its loyal base.

How? Fortunately for you, one of the authors was a sucker for book retailer Borders' weekly discount vouchers and bought the entire series because of the design of the cover (thereby proving the adage of never judge a book by its cover). In the books, vampire love interest Edward drives a Volvo (not the most obvious choice, but these vamps really are on the dull side). Being possessed of supernatural senses he can safely drive like a demon, which is just as well for his very human love interest, the perpetually moping Bella. Volvo did a tie in with the movie release. Meyer's choice of vehicle was probably calculated, but for Volvo it was perfect. Edward's most treasured possession in the whole world was Bella, and what better brand than Volvo to keep her safe while he showed off. The campaign did several things. First, Volvo appeals primarily to women drivers. Twilight ensured the brand was introduced to a younger audience while also appealing to older women who also loved the series. The campaign played on the brand's historic emphasis on safety (i.e., distinctiveness), while being updated in a very on-brand way. Even cultural branders would have grudgingly approved of the connection.

While the arguments between those advocating difference and distinctiveness can get heated, both sides largely agree on the importance of being meaningful to consumers. Distinctiveness advocates do not talk much about positioning (they tend to focus on tactics more), but their call for brand managers to focus on what their brand is known and valued for is really an indirect (via brand image) reflection of position. For those advocating difference, it's a bit trickier. Positioning involves seeking a sweet spot between relevance, competitive difference, and deliverability. The problem is too much emphasis goes on difference. If you do positioning right (see later on this chapter), you start with relevance and that then guides the whole process (only competitors offering differences that are relevant matter, while only capabilities that deliver relevance are useful). Both sides are essentially talking past one another, unless one is advocating for an USP.

segments: selling to everyone or selecting a few

If you're familiar with marketing, no doubt you will know about the idea of segmentation. But as a quick refresh, segmentation involves splitting the market up into distinct groups of consumers who share the same characteristics. This practice has long underpinned branding, from the process of segmentation – targeting – positioning through to extending the brand to reach underserved groups of consumers. Segmentation requires brand managers to focus on 'their' target group of consumers. As such, one must be careful not to confuse the views of your target group with those of the general public, online activists, self-declared experts and others. Nike, for example, has engaged in brand activism with the 2019 Dream Crazy campaign seemingly around #blacklivesmatter not to bring people together or improve race relations, but to affirm the brand's political credentials with their target market that skews (at least in the United States) young and center-left politically. Images circulating online of right wingers burning their shoes in disgust should not cause the Nike brand team to bat an eyelid. They revel in becoming a more divisive brand in political terms, especially when it results in an uptick in sales of 35%.

But do segments actually exist? Much of the controversy around segmentation has concerned the basis on which it is done – do you use demographics (no), psychographics (no) or behavior (probably a good idea)? However, despite segmentation, particularly in the form of cohort groups (Generation X/Y/Z/<insert letter of choice>, Millennials, and so on) being part of everyday usage, marketing researchers have often struggled to find meaningful differences between purchasers of brands (outside of the obvious such as luxury brands being purchased by those with higher incomes). Segments seem to be something we try and impose on unruly markets rather than representing genuine differences in behavior (Sharp 2010). If segments do not exist, what does this mean for brand management?

In branding, the debate over the existence of segments has given rise to a renewed emphasis on mass marketing rather than targeted marketing as a strategy for brand growth. Although recently driven by the Ehrenberg–Bass folks, questions over the existence of segments go back some way. Some cynics have noted that Ehrenberg–Bass have not been averse to using segmentation, benefitting from targeting senior marketing managers at large fast-moving consumer goods (FMCG) firms to gain support for their ideas. In fairness, there is a difference between dividing up markets and developing specialist brand marketing messages or even separate brands for each and looking to gain the support of influential supporters for your ideas (when it comes to ideas and influence, the process is a political one).

For those calling for mass marketing, segments get in the way of brand growth, are at best inefficient and at worse, self-defeating. Targeting as many buyers as one can, particularly lighter or non-users is a way to keep renewing the rapidly depleting loyal customer base. More is always better, as long as growth does not rely on price promotion (which can damage brand image in the long run). Making it easier to find your brand through mass distribution, and being clear about distinctive benefits is the path to growth.

Those who argue against this represent many different perspectives. Some simply argue on the basis of pragmatism. For smaller firms or organizations not facing and endless need for growth (you'd think universities too but tell that to a vice chancellor who receives bonuses for recruitment growth), targeting your marketing toward a specific audience is an effective use of limited marketing resources while also sending a signal about intent. Others draw on (often carefully constructed) case studies of brands that have benefitted from targeted marketing, arguing that making brands more exclusive, for example, is essential to their desirability. However, luxury brands are often far less exclusive in practice than their image and associated mythology would imply, using an array of mass-marketing tools such as lower cost products (perfumes, key rings, wallets, etc.) to feed the so-called democratization or massification of luxury, while at the same time relying on cultural associations with the rich and famous and some very expensive limited releases to maintain a halo effect for the brand.

Those arguing for mass marketing also downplay the power of a brand's image. It is probably true that consumers of baked beans or colas are not that different, but other brands have become very adept at being associated with a set of images. Toyota's mass-market appeal of offering great value for money proved less appealing when the marque was trying to enter higher priced, luxury segments where status matters. Testing revealed consumers had no doubts about the reliability and performance of potential luxury Toyota, but such a utilitarian image was decidedly off-putting as a signal of 'having made it'. The brand could only stretch so far, which is why the Toyota owned and produced Lexus brand came to exist. There are plenty of other examples of the limited ability of brands to appeal to as many consumers as possible. Also, while segments may not really exist, they remain real for many key business buyers such as channel partners, which make gaining listings for your mass-appeal fashion brand in the coolest inner-city stores much harder.

So where does this leave us? For new brands, Passionbrand's Helen Edwards offers her usual practical wisdom, to target a segment as a starting point and keep an open mind when it comes to mass appeal. Cultural branders often do not concern themselves with pragmatic issues but for segments they do talk about developing a target and follower brief as a means of achieving growth (their research is typically based in iconic mass brands). Brand image may place a brake on how fast or far a brand can go, and consumer centricity demands those limits be respected. A new brand may be the answer here, but one can also carefully curate a selection of collaborators (which may include a host of other brands) who may help shift meaning or provide the authenticity necessary to tap into new audiences.

brand audits: can you walk the walk?

Ever heard the phrase 'on-brand'? A seemingly meaningless statement that all too often clouds one's judgement when being decidedly off-brand is the right thing to do, it nevertheless does reflect a foundation principle of branding – that brands are built from the inside out. Although many people associate brands with logos or various forms of communications, our actual experience of brands, be it smooth or rough, reflects the work that goes into aligning all aspects of the firm in such a way as to deliver on the brand's promise consistently over time. The process behind this is known as the dreaded brand audit.

So what is to be aligned? Corporate branding researchers talk about three gaps that can potentially emerge between the brand team, external stakeholders, and employees. Hatch and Schultz (2001) refer to these in their *Harvard Business Review* article 'Are your corporate brand stars aligned?' which as the title suggests, is focused on the potential cosmic karma that comes from aligned planets. The authors focus on the gaps between how the brand team view the brand (i.e., its identity), how external stakeholders see the brand (i.e., its image), and how employees view the brand (i.e., its culture). This result in three key gaps to be aligned: identity–image, identity–culture, and image–culture. Each is in effect addressed in a brand audit.

The identity–image gap is the one most brand marketers will be familiar with, as it concerns the gap between what you would like the brand to be and how external stakeholders view it. Most of the work one does in tracking customers' views of the brand relates to this gap. Your ultimate goal is aligning identity and image as this will make your communications more efficient and also mean you are achieving your strategic objectives. The complication that Hatch and Schultz (2008) add is that they do not privilege customer views but expand it to include stakeholders. Part of this relates to the power of some stakeholders, such as shareholders, to influence image and even identity (as many large corporates investing in brand purpose have found). However, it is also the recognition that one stakeholder can influence the other, helping to shape brand image. For example, if activists criticize a brand for its impact on the environment, this may influence how consumers see the brand's image, thereby increasing the gap between identity and image.

The identity–culture gap relates to the potential for misalignment between the brand's aspirational values and how employees see the brand, or the experience they have within the company per se. This partly is why as employees we are bombarded with staff satisfaction and engagement surveys to ensure we both understand and even appreciate the core values of the firm and brand. This also reflects the idea that if the brand is built from the inside-out, then ensuring we have engaged, contented employees who are trained, equipped, and rewarded to reinforce the brand's position are essential. One of the pioneers of internal branding is US low-cost airline Southwest Airlines (Miles and Mangold 2005). The founder, Herb Kelleher has stated that taking care of employees is all one needs to do to build the brand. This is of course a simplification, but his logic has a ring of truth to it. The brand's hiring practices look for non-traditional airline employees, stressing that all staff must be focused on getting the plane away on time (pilots may be expected to help out in the cabin if they can), and to get customers to play their part in getting seated quickly and also putting bags in lockers. This often means spontaneity, entertainment ability, and emotional labor are essential hiring factors.

The image–culture gap relates to potential conflict between employees and external stakeholders. There are a number of influences at work here. One is that in many services organizations customer loyalty to particular employees has a positive spillover for the brand (Macintosh and Lockshin 1997). Another is that employees may become admired or despised by stakeholders. One classical example is the use of buff models as staff by Abercrombie & Fitch (or Abercrombie & Snitch, depending on your view), which reinforced the brand's in-group image with customers while also earning the ire of disability rights advocates who felt it was exclusionary (the latter won out in the end, ensuring the brand became decidedly uncool with its target group).

One example of brands suffering from alignment gaps comes from the ethically positioned Body Shop. The brand, which at the time of writing is in serious decline, was built around the values of founder Anita Roddick who believed commerce could be a force for good. The original stores championed a range of primarily center-left political positions including fair pay, environmental sustainability, support for minority groups, and being against animal testing. The products were made with natural ingredients that were harvested sustainably. The brand was a hit, and global expansion beckoned. In the United States, however, the brand ran into trouble. The United States is a difficult market because expansion often has to happen very quickly, to respond to consumer demand and potential competitor imitation. For retailers this is particularly tricky because one must secure sites and ramp up production, and, critically, employ staff. The Body Shop's problems arose because the team did not focus on aligning new employees with their values, nor support them effectively, resulting in public complaints of bullying, racism, and poor customer service, all of which were at odds with their values. The brand only started to turnaround when this identity–culture gap was addressed (Beverland 2009).

Brand audits basically are aimed at ensuring you can walk the walk as well as talk the talk. Those writing on brand authenticity argue this is the most basic form of keeping it real, authenticity as consistency. Once one has decided the brand's position, the first step is to examine how the organization stacks up against its aspiration. Not for nothing did Naomi Klein (2000) get under the skin of brand managers with *No Logo* when she in effect compared their high-minded aspirations with the reality of their practices, particularly those on the environment and the treatment of workers in offshore factories. Saying your brand is all about 'being the best you' is all well and good, but it isn't a good look when the firm's practices suggest do as we say not do as we do. *No Logo* had a real effect, precisely because Klein understood branding, needling brand managers right where it hurt.

So what happens in a brand audit? Basically you examine everything you do and compare it with your brand position. You may use staff as proxy mystery consumers to understand the customer's journey or their experience when interacting with your organization. Surveying stakeholders and staff is critical. Working with human resources to train staff in ways that reinforce the brand position also ensures engagement with the brand, and highlights areas for process improvement. Looking at your products, services, influencers, partners, suppliers and their practices, and so on is also part of the process. Basically, since your brand represents a promise to the consumer, you need to be sure you can deliver on it, each and every time they deal with you.

Such audits also have implications for some of the enduring challenges within branding covered in the next chapter. In relation to the branding of cities or places, the brand audit logic would focus on what you need to add (all too often the things that excite Richard Florida's (2002) much-maligned creative class) and what you may need to remove. Think about the ethics of that for a second. Olympic hosts regularly try and move on homeless people as part of this brand logic. What might work for products and services probably shouldn't for places (unless you are a dictator, but then you'll already have mastered the removal process). Likewise with purpose, for all the supportive statements by big brands during the 2020 #blacklivesmatter protests, it didn't take brand journalists long to juxtapose them against the photos of an all-white, mostly male, corporate board (Ritson 2020b).

living the brand

A colleague of ours undertakes corporate tours whereby experienced professions visit particular companies overseas to get exposure to new ideas in practice. It's a nice corporate junket and also can be written off against tax. One participant described to us how they watched with bemusement a Nike employee literally transform themselves before their eyes into a walking, talking billboard for the brand. As soon as they realized they were hosting the party of tourists, their whole demeanor and tone of voice changed. In a way they were the human embodiment of the brand (the more critically minded may see this in much darker terms).

The idea that one should live the brand is fairly common among corporates today (Ind 2014), especially for employees in customer facing roles. Whereas the paternalistic capitalists of the industrial revolution tried to control their employees' behavior through a mix of carrot and stick, housing them often in branded communities subject to strict moral guidelines (that often had nothing to do with the firm's values), modern organizations try to get employees to embody certain values, often represented by that innocuous phrase 'organizational culture'.

William Whyte coined the phrase 'the organization man' when he wrote his 1956 corporate classic of the same name. The logic here was that employees could come together as a collective, think and act alike, for the good of the company (and by implication themselves). Massively influential on corporate practice, the idea became popularized in the 1980s as corporate culture which was simply defined as 'the way we do things around here' (Deal and Kennedy 1982). However, the idea has slightly more ominous roots, including the ideological purism of those early 20th century masters of branding, such as the Nazis and Soviets who held that fealty to the party and its ideology was essential to being a good citizen (and indeed a living one) (Heller 2008). They did this through an array of rituals, uniforms, slogans, status awards, boot-camps, and if one strayed, re-education facilities.

Foucault, in his 1977 study of prisons, noted that the historic design of the panopticon was the ideal system because prisoners essentially acted as if they were watched all the time, which had the impact of not requiring direct control. Neoliberalism builds on this, looking for ways to have employees voluntarily adopt an ideology of agency and self-responsibility that sees them monitor their own actions and that of others to ensure they work hard for the corporation. More recently, studies of social media influencers identify how the logic of personal branding with all its tracking data and emphasis on engagement metrics ensures control while also allowing the influencer to maintain the belief they are being true to themselves (Heeris Christensen et al. 2024).

Some organizations embody this as a way of ensuring high standards of performance. One large global airline is known for turning all its staff into snitches, rewarding them for reporting infractions against brand rules. This does ensure some performance but also creates a climate of fear. These types of service organizations encourage what is called 'emotional labor' in which employees are encouraged to present their best selves to the customer, downplaying their authentic selves and staying resolutely on a customer-centric branded script. Influencers, particularly those that do not enjoy the power of celebrity, have such a precarious existence (low entry barriers, little real differentiation, and fickle followers) that they have it even worse than airline staff. They are rewarded for playing up their authentic self as that is their brand promise. No personal misery is off limits for a fanbase that feeds on emotional pain out of the belief that it makes their brand of choice 'real' (Heeris Christensen et al. 2024).

Beyond control however, there is a practical reason for the living the brand mantra. One common mistake in branding is you start with communications or logos, etc., and then build the brand relationship with the consumer. In practice, this usually leads to disaster as you have not prepared the way for the promise at the heart of your brand to be delivered consistently every time. Experienced brand professionals therefore talk about building the brand from the inside out. This is the reason for the brand audit process we cover in this chapter, but it also gives rise to a focus on internal branding, or the process of embedding brand values in the organization's culture.

Internal branding is an offshoot of what was briefly called internal marketing and was aimed at overcoming the problems that arose from branding or marketing being siloed within disciplinary boundaries. Just as it was once said that capitalism was too important to be left to the capitalists, marketing, and branding were too important to be left solely in the hands of their practitioners. Whereas for manufacturing firms, workers may need little knowledge of the brand, in service organizations, understanding the brand is essential as every encounter one has with customers is known as a 'moment of truth' where, much like the US gameshow *Moment of Truth*, the brand's core claim(s) are under the spotlight.

Internal branding is often underappreciated, but it does allow two of the more important and least appreciated parts of the organization to work more closely together. As we have discussed elsewhere, there are many non-customer benefits of branding, and integrating human resources with brand marketing provides many of those, including the ability to enhance employer brand equity. However, internal branding goes further than just the provision of training and the much maligned 'brand identity guide'. The latter are often slickly produced but intellectually dull guides on how to use the brand's much-loved assets (well, much-loved by marketers anyway). Marketers rarely know how much these guides are despised but if they start picking up on the phrase 'brand police' they should get worried, as the brand has become associated solely with the color and font of a PowerPoint slide. That said, these guides are necessary to ensure consistency of application, but absent any presentation and engagement with the brand's position and identity, they are of little use. And it often doesn't hurt to provide some options for different divisions.

One example of this is the shift at Yamaha Music to a one-brand identity. Historically, the company allowed each division the right to market the brand as it saw fit. There was some logic to this, albeit mistaken. Each division was of the view that their customers were unique, and, importantly, didn't like the customers of other divisions. Thus, mild-mannered, well-dressed classical musicians did not want to be reminded that the company made guitars for hotel-room-trashing, hard-living rockers or street-smart DJs on speed doing an all-night rave. Turns out that the marketing managers were wrong, and musicians, like the rest of us, have more in common with each other, enjoying different genres and even working across genre boundaries. The company was missing out on the power and efficiency of one strong brand built around shared values. But to make this happen, skeptical divisional managers needed to be convinced through research, needed a shared brand identity they could engage with, and needed the ability to adjust some of the assets to work more effectively in particular settings. All of this did happen and reflected the ways in which internal branding can build engagement among staff and particularly more powerful managers who will champion brand investment on your behalf.

Internal branding therefore helps close those alignment gaps we saw earlier, but should be viewed as a collaborative process, whereby staff are engaged in the development and diffusion of brand strategy. What this doesn't mean is lecturing to them or making them suffer through awaydays packed with Post-it Note design thinking, diary-ing their thoughts, LEGO building, and so on. Instead, listening to employees and engaging them in strategy development helps ground the brand in the authenticity or lived tradition of people who often care deeply about their work and the company they have been at far longer than high-turnover brand managers. Seminal examinations of this at some of Denmark's largest firms, including Bang & Olufsen and Carlsberg have identified how employee ownership of brand revitalization ensured that brand traditions were blended with market requirements, resulting in alignment between identity, image, and culture, but also reinforcement of each brand's distinctive image in the market (Hatch and Schultz 2008, 2017).

brand research and metrics

You know it was coming. At some point in any marketing course, you are going to have to deal with the boring stuff. Or maybe not. One of our former executive MBA students (who was also the founder of a cut-price advertising agency) once told us that his job was mainly to ensure that he had free parking for his creatives' Porsches and free coke (yep that kind) to stimulate their creativity. When we discussed the research into brand positioning, his answer was well, mostly the brand idea came in the form of something scribbled on a business card that had been used by the creatives to cut said narcotic. Even though our student was notorious for taking the piss, we both sensed there was some truth to this and subsequent retellings have us convinced.

But, in all seriousness, marketing, and by implication branding, requires market data, and that means research. Fortunately for you, and frankly for us, we are not about to write a market research book replete with statistical details (both of us are senior academics and beyond that type of grunt work). But where to start? Since we want you to be brand experts (even if only performatively), let's look at what you do need and when. Methods, especially those for tracking things like engagement are shifting all the time, especially as we move into the world of AI or artificial intelligence (which has the potential to inject the term 'meticulous' into any conversation), which is already being widely adopted by brand teams, with little realization that they are sealing their own fate (for university marketing teams, AI will continue to ensure vapid campaigns and the same tedious taglines about changing the world).

Let's break this up into research that you need for brand building, research you need for brand activation, and research you need to measure your impact (we won't say success because that would be presumptuous, young Padawans). There are some critical lessons that go across all these situations. First, forget pointless debates regarding qualitative versus quantitative. You will need both, always. Second, remember that your brand is always positioned within a category, which means data, for the most part, needs to be comparative. Third, insights are vital. You must use them, not cherry pick them, and not try and save money by contacting people like us with a 'really good idea for a student project'. Finally, make sure you measure performance, in real terms, otherwise the finance folk might start looking closely at your budget, which will start them asking about those regular cash payments for 'creative supplements'.

Let's start with research around brand identity, which can involve building a new brand from scratch, leveraging the reputation of an existing firm into a brand, or even seeking to inject life and power into a tired brand. In each case you will need research to identify your possible segments, including who they are, how large each is, and their potential. Behavioral information is best here as demographics is not useful for distinguishing meaningful differences. That means stop babbling about the cohort of the day – while constantly talking about generation this or that may create a lot of value for specialist consultants, there has never been any data to support their existence. Demographics are useful for activations however, as the information can be useful for identifying where to advertise, design features, who to feature in your advertisements, and so on (all of which are tactical, rather than strategic, decisions).

At some point you will need to go deep, which can involve ethnographic research, in-depth interviews, or projective techniques that help get inside the target's subconscious. In each case, you want to understand how the target user sees your brand or organization. Yamaha, for example, asked young musicians to draw the brand. The result was telling – a serious old man who never smiled. Interviews identified that the brand was admired for its quality but didn't capture the emotion of making music. These powerful images (supported by quantitative research) were essential for moving the company away from product-centric marketing driven by separate divisions to one singular brand strategy that was emotional in content.

These types of projective techniques help get at the subconscious and are popular with brand managers and often misused. One of the most thorough is the crisply named Zaltman Metaphor Elicitation Technique (ZMET). Named after its inventor, Harvard professor Gerald Zaltman (2003), the technique asks respondents to compare and contrast images around an idea in order to get a better understanding of their personality or identity, or of an idea like authenticity. One of us used this to develop our insights into brand authenticity, getting consumers to bring in images they associated with authenticity and inauthenticity. Basically you annoy the hell out of consumers by asking them what each image is about, and how it is similar to and different from that other one, and you keep doing it through multiple rounds (academically we'd say we stop when theoretical saturation occurs but in practice its usually when the interviewees' annoyance threshold is reached and they throw something at you). Sometimes just asking them to draw something or make a collage is easier, but the idea is the same, using something to elicit deeper ideas that are hard to explain verbally or consciously.

Once you have your basic ideas around your brand, good and bad, you can develop these as scales and measure. This is why the qualitative vs. quantitative data is pointless – the latter builds on the former and done well, helps tighten and clarify. Qualitative research is about discovery and exploration, quantitative is about testing and precision. Anyone who dismisses one, or just has a preference for one particular tool, including those bores who only love 'social' (or social media for the uninitiated), design thinkers who dismiss consumer research because 'Apple never did market research' (one of the many myths that are largely false, repeated by marketers who should know better), the quant bores who hate what they see as 'just stories' or the manager who cherry picked one comment from a focus group because it confirms their bias (this is common so as brand manager, always chaperone senior managers and distract them with a mirror and possibly alcohol), should be harshly slapped.

When it's time to execute, pre-testing is essential. People will disagree with us here, but it is so easy to pre-test ideas with simple analog or digital tools to get some last-minute feedback that may make all the difference. This is where focus groups can be very useful, but there are also a range of simple crowdsourcing tools that can be used to gain feedback on options and even indicators of preferences. And you can get those insights quickly and at scale.

After that the focus moves into the quantitative domain and can include a whole host of standardized and ad hoc tools depending on your needs. The standardized tools typically involve larger scale surveys of consumers on your brand image, and also tracking, which is largely a check on whether your marketing is landing the way you hoped. Other tools may involve measures of engagement, which can be as simple as tracking responses to individual social media posts, through to social media mentions of the brand both in terms of numbers and content. For the latter it is important to have a clear understanding of competitive benchmarks, or at least an understanding of the size of your audience. Too often we have sat through marketing meetings with engagement levels in the single digits being reported as performance metrics (without any sense of shame) despite an audience size ranging in the hundreds of thousands.

Other measures also include examinations of the impact of our brand marketing. Share of voice, for example, looks at the effectiveness of our advertising and whether our messages are cutting through against those of our competitors. Although often regarded as something of a holy grail among marketers, there are some assumptions made in calculating this metric and identifying who your audience is and the impact of your advertising on their responses is often trickier than you think. Mark Ritson (2020a), who was long a champion of share of voice has recently suggested that share of search might be a better measure because it is generated by consumers, is already some way down marketing's famous funnel, and is a mix of behavior (the actual search) and associations (the content of that search). Therefore, it may be a useful measure of tracking brand image. Share of search potentially may become more popular, particularly as large search engine brands open up their data for commercial exploitation and can provide a useful tool for tracking search combinations, identifying desired (and less desired) associations, new leads, and, of course, possible shifts in your brand's meaning.

As mentioned earlier, tracking is an essential brand tool, and it simply involves regular measurement of your brand's desired position relative to other brands occupying the same segment or appealing to the same need. These data are essential because they provide you with evidence your marketing is working and that you have points of difference and/or distinctiveness, while also highlighting potential associations you could acquire to enhance your brand's meaning without sacrificing existing ones. Tracking also helps act as an early warning system for problems, often identifying when those points of difference are becoming parities in the market. Fortunately, tracking is very much a standardized tool, so although an essential investment, prices tend to be competitive.

Ad hoc tools typically require more specialized help and as the term suggests, depend very much on the problem to be solved. Examples may include using things like conjoint analysis to examine consumer sensitivity where trade-offs are involved (price vs. quality or functionality, for example) or experimentation where you are looking to understand particular decision-making processes. Word of warning — be prepared for eye-watering costs from specialist agencies in the case of ad hoc work!

getting to the top of the pyramid: what is all this stuff about awareness, top-of-mind, and salience?

Tracking is useful right? Go on, admit it, you like tracking the progress of your parcel from shipper to the door. Far better than relying on random postal deliveries or estimates. Knowing where something is and when it might arrive provides useful information, and having the ability to change delivery time and place provides a sense of control or agency. Alright, it's not the best analogy, but no one employed us for our creative insights. Needless to say, brand managers (at least those who deserve the title) also spend time and money on tracking. So what do they track and why?

Tracking is one of the more important, yet most mundane and often underappreciated, activities in brand management. Since brands require often substantial investment, particularly in communications, we need some insight into how effective that spend is (if we want to keep getting more cash from the finance director, that is). Tracking also demonstrates if we are building connections with our consumers, if those connections are getting stronger or weaker, and if we are doing it better than our competitors. This is why brand teams ruminate over archaic measures such as 'top-of-mind', 'aided recall', and so on.

Given the centrality of customer knowledge to building brand equity, marketers spend time measuring the strength and depth of knowledge. Since marketers never really escaped the misreading of Maslow's so-called hierarchy of needs, we remain wedded to pyramids and with their cumulative steps of development toward nirvana. This is reflected in how we track consumer awareness of the brand. Lest you think awareness just means what it says, marketers break awareness into a set of stages, which they measure with reference to different levels.

The first two measures that will matter to you are those of aided and unaided recall. Marketing researchers, after controlling for relevance of a category or need to you, usually ask two questions: 'list all the brands of category X you know', and then 'are you aware of the following brands?' (providing names or images of each, which of course are usually their clients). What are they getting at? The first question measures unaided recall, which is assumed to reflect a deeper level of brand knowledge because you already know it serves a particular need or exists in a specific category and has some benefits. It is likely you have trialled the brand and that it fits within your 'consideration set', which is the group of 4-5 brands already saved in your computer-like mind that you are prepared to buy from within a category. The second question relates to aided recall (which taps into a lower level of knowledge), trying to measure if some awareness of the brand is already built, primarily through communications and possibly retail reach. Both matter of course, but conversion from aided to unaided really gets marketers excited (they really are a sad bunch at times).

The next step on the pyramid represents a further step toward brand nirvana. This is called top-of mind-awareness and is simply a measure of how many consumers list your brand first in the unaided recall exercise. Try it yourself, pick a category where you select from several brands (so not something like banking where we know switching is rare) and just list the brands that come to mind. Is the first your favorite? Top-of-mind awareness reflects what Marty Neumeier calls the 'gut feel' of branding, or your preference. Since you automatically put it down, it captures your unconscious preference, which is formed primarily through interaction or behavior over many months and maybe years. When we collate percentages of top-of-mind awareness we often get a very good approximate measure of market share, which is why marketers obsess (often too much) over conversions from unaided recall to top-of-mind.

All this emphasis on conversion sounds good. But it does cost, and in light of data that suggests loyalty is more fleeting, sometimes the cost outweighs the benefit. Getting from aided to unaided matters, but simply increasing your percentage of unaided recall among consumers may be more valuable than trying to maximize top-of-mind. There's a further danger to reaching the pinnacle of the pyramid, and it isn't the obvious truism that the only way is down. One can have too much top-of-mind, which often means you are ubiquitous and synonymous with the category.

To give you an example, we wrote a tongue-in-cheek article on the Phil Collins Effect (Spicer et al. 2022), named after the brilliant drummer from prog-rock band Genesis, favorite artist of Bret Easton Ellis' *American Psycho* Patrick Bateman (also a poster boy for brands and the extended self), and everyman 1980s popstar. Best known for the song 'In the Air Tonight' (its gated reverb drum track so recognizable that Cadbury used it a much-loved advertising campaign, except they replaced Collins with a gorilla on the drums), Collins suffered in the late 1980s from too much exposure. One literally could not avoid his music, and this oversaturation led to contempt (it didn't help that Collins was rather curmudgeonly about any criticism).

Much the same can happen with some brands, particularly those which are first movers into a category, such as Hoover for vacuum cleaners (ask your parents), or Johnson & Johnson with Band-aids, 3M for Post-it Notes or indeed Google for search engines. Their dominance comes from a combination of addressing an unmet need extremely well, mass availability, and price competitiveness. But there's a problem. Like Phil Collins being representative of 'muzak', the ubiquity of these brands means they become synonymous with that category, hence we ask for a Band-aid or decide to Google it, regardless of whether we are using the origin brand or not. Over time, as patents expire, this leads the original brand to become a commodity and low-cost followers take share. Too much of top-of-mind is a double-edged sword, with familiarity with brand benefit breeding indifference to the brand. And, unlike Collins, there may be no chance of a bounce back.

One way to avoid all this of course is innovation. To leverage the equity of say a breakthrough product, such as a search engine to expand into devices to search (phones), or a band-aid to create a broader platform around emergency medical care one can trust. That is, one must extend the brand, to add extra layers of meaning.

do you need a brand extension?

You may already have cottoned on to the importance of keeping the brand fresh or relevant (if you haven't it's not our fault). Likewise, to the importance of growth. One approach for achieving both is brand extension. Every year *schadenfreude* is directed at clueless marketers who engage in 'what were they thinking' brand extensions, be it motorcycle brands offering perfumes, car brands selling flame throwers, or makers of disposable cigarette lighters deciding that their brand benefits can extend into underwear and yes, perfume (at some point it always comes down to perfume).

Other self-declared experts lambast stupid brand managers for failing to understand their true brand heritage or image, when they take their brand into different markets. So bad are these extensions that the death of the parent brand is claimed to be just around the corner. Since this rarely comes to pass, one wonders why such experts never seem to learn. Brand extension is one thing that everyone has an opinion on, and few get right. Unfortunately, brand extension is also essential for building brand equity.

So why do so many people get brand extension wrong? The naysayers tend to confuse two types of extension: line and category. The first has a higher chance of success and largely just involves adding variants (such as new flavors) or going up or down the price curve. The second, has a higher chance of failure, and involves taking the brand into entirely new categories, such as taking a record label brand into airlines and then into cola, and so on. Each extension can enhance the brand being extended (i.e., the parent brand), but only one can really damage it when things go wrong. Everyone makes the same mistake, arguing that category extensions that fail are the most dangerous, but in reality, since the bar is set so low in terms of expectation, these extensions may waste money but do no harm to the parent brand. No one after all expects a couture brand to master a mobile phone, or an airline to be good at bridal wear. However, when the low-risk line extension goes wrong, this makes people wonder about your expertise.

Now that's out of the way, how do extensions work? Well, it's all about fit. The late Johnnie Cochran, the lawyer who managed to get (the also late) OJ Simpson acquitted of murdering his wife and her friend famously said, 'if the gloves don't fit, you must acquit' and in a way this describes the underpinning logic of extension. The psychologically minded essentially test whether consumers see some degree of congruence between the parent brand and the extension. This may involve complementarity, for example, such as whether a brand of toothpaste could move into other areas of dental care, or whether a heavy machinery brand could make work wear. The culturally minded focus on the extension's authenticity, looking less as congruence and more at sincerity of intent (i.e., what motivates the brand team in moving into tangential or oppositional categories?) (Spiggle et al. 2012). While some might question whether ethical fashion brands can extend into fast fashion, often through a collaboration, it may all come down to how the designer behind the parent frames their motives (perhaps some disingenuous desire to convince consumers that fast fashion needn't be cheap and disposable, which of course is the very *raison d'etre* of the category).

So, don't be afraid to extend, but do your research, and make sure the gloves fit or if they don't, at least argue that your intent is sincere (even if it's not).

brand architecture: a tale of two houses

What has architecture got to do with branding you ask? Well, apart from a late 1990s short-term investment in iconic high-end brand flagship stores that were designed to immerse customers in the very essence of the brand (without being so crass as to encourage you to buy anything), thankfully not much. But the term is a useful metaphor for capturing how firms organize their brand portfolios. As a result, you need to familiarize yourself with the difference between a branded house and a house of brands.

Organizations such as Procter & Gamble, Unilever, Mars, and L'Oréal have had a significant influence on brand management practice. Dealing with what are referred to as FMCGs (or fast-moving consumer goods, those relatively low-cost essentials we buy a lot of, usually from supermarkets), these organizations used multiple brands to fuel their growth. Why? Procter & Gamble realized that brands often reached a natural peak in growth, whereby trying to attract more consumers could only come from dragging them away from brands they were happy with. This was either too costly or seen as futile. So, they decided to acquire the brands that had the temerity to stand in their way and as such gained customers and share by stealth. They quickly realized that growth could come from owning multiple brands in the same category. The house of brands was born.

The house of brands approach is popular in many product categories, from the mundane to the luxurious, and enables you to offer the appearance of choice to consumers (try it sometime, go to a category in a supermarket, select three different brands of any category (deodorant, cleaner, pet food, etc.) and check for the small print identifying true ownership), adopt radically different identities within your portfolio (that appeal to different users), and avoid any contamination that might arise from a scandal in one brand. Retailers also benefit because they can deal with one supplier, which saves time and allows for a more strategic relationship. There are some costs. The strategy is inefficient as you need separate marketing for each brand, and it can make cross-selling impossible.

Although these limitations are real, it may be best to simply live with them and be ruthless in managing your portfolio, reducing the number of brands in saturated categories and investing in growth areas, while also putting more resources behind your large brands. Too often marketers make the mistake that consumers are deeply impressed by the size of your portfolio and decide to wow them with the huge scope of what they have to offer. But consumers are not (always) viewers of pornography, that is, they may actually be turned off by the size and content of your portfolio. No fine wine drinker wants to know that your portfolio also includes a big-selling, mediocre lager (and we'd wager that the opposite is true). Likewise, no dog owner wants to know the maker of their preferred pet food also makes the dog poison that is chocolate (we're not taking bets on whether the opposite is also true). When dealing with consumers, keep your portfolio to yourself; you'll have plenty of time to brag about it to other marketers over drinks at conferences.

Is there an alternative? Typically consumer and business services companies prefer one 'master' brand. This strategy is the branded house. Why? Such an approach allows service organizations such as banks and universities to offer a range of services through the lifetime of the consumer or business customer and adapt these as needs change. There's no point in having a portfolio of banks, for example, each offering specialist services, if you can have one bank with different divisions that can address complex needs. Such strategies appeal to the wannabe dictator inside of all brand managers, as it allows them to grow their empire, burning their mark into more and more territory as they go. And as long as nothing goes wrong, the strategy has merits.

And therein lies the rub, branded houses are great for efficiency, cross-selling, and sheer power, but you have to be on your game because there is nowhere to hide if something goes wrong in one part of the business. Whereas a house of brands can contain any damage to one brand, a branded house cannot. This is not a reason to avoid this approach, just something to be aware of. Each strategy has strengths and weaknesses, and each can be modified through a variety of co-naming options such as endorsements, shadow endorsements, and so on, all of which are covered by the famous brand relationship spectrum by David Aaker and Erich Joachimsthaler (2000).

who doesn't love a story? communicating without selling

Historically many advertisers (and advertising used to be the main form of brand marketing) always designed messages with a call to action. This is where the idea of the 'hard sell' came from. The logic of this was pretty simple. Marketers believe in something called a funnel, which of course looks like a three-dimensional pyramid, so is instantly attractive. The marketing funnel is based on the logic of a hierarchy of effects, and it basically holds that consumers go through different stages in their decision-making processes. Specifically, they move from a state of ignorance through to awareness, greater interest, consideration, to conversion, and return. The role of marketing communications is to help consumers move from one stage to the next, if we are to make a sale and subsequently get them to return and buy again.

This logic has some intuitive appeal, it actually doesn't have much empirical support and assumes consumers are far more rational than they are. So the funnel went out of fashion for a while, but it seems to be back in business, largely because marketers like it. It now has a host of variations, but the logic remains the same – marketers must adapt their communications to each decision-making stage so that the potential consumer or lead becomes a loyal one.

What does this have to do with storytelling? Well nothing in a way, but also everything. As ex-advertising planner and retired University of Bath professor Robert Heath (2001) wrote in his PhD dissertation, *The Hidden Power of Advertising* (which became an industry best seller), the whole emphasis on a call to action is based on the assumption that consumers pay attention to advertising. Ruthlessly unpicking many of the ways in which experimental studies ensured their subjects actually did attend to advertising, he found that this assumption just did not stack up, neither psychologically nor empirically. But he did find, and demonstrated through his own campaign successes, that advertising had hidden powers of persuasion. Rather than a call to action, advertisements should feature few words, and simply create emotional resonance. That is, by appearing not to be an actual advert (usually through short stories), consumers' subconscious would be more open to building associations and feelings toward the brand. Heath called this low-attention processing and much like Sharp's work on brand growth, he initially had a greater impact in practice than academia (although this has since changed). Heath's monograph is out of print, but his subsequent book *Seducing the Subconscious* (2012) is a must-have.

All of this underpins the newfound interest in storytelling as an effective form of brand marketing communications (it is also immensely effective for internal brand training purposes and is perhaps why students love to hear from practitioners as they recount their 'war stories' from the field). Storytelling is also seen as a way to build greater emotional resonance with the brand, or in this age of brand authenticity, brand sentiment, which captures how consumers and others talk, feel, and behave toward the brand. Stories are also universal. Christopher Booker (2004) suggests there are seven basic plots (in his book of the same name) across all cultures and narrative forms of art. Brands have embraced many of these including overcoming the monster, rags to riches, the quest, voyage and return, comedy and tragedy, and rebirth. Booker's is by no means an exhaustive list, but the point is that storytelling is a universal form of sensemaking across cultures.

David Aaker (2018) writes about signature stories as a means to clarify brand position and provide the brand with energy and visibility among consumers and even employees. These are stories that the brand can authentically own and may involve the enduring values of the founder or innovator behind the brand, great service encounters, or consumer moments. Tom van Laer at the University of Technology Sydney is one of the foremost authorities of how storytelling works in marketing. Van Laer et al. (2014) identify a process called 'narrative transportation' as essential to story success. What this means is that when consumers can insert themselves into the narrative of the brand, then by definition they identify with the brand and the story has done its job.

An example from a serial brand, *Survivor*, will illustrate. *Survivor* was a successful reality television show where contestants were put on an island in the middle of nowhere and competed for survival (and obviously some prizes). Of course, the brand team behind the show didn't just pick contestants at random, rather they picked contestants that would get under each other's skin. Some had skills, some were beautiful, some were older, and some younger. For the competition to be engaging, contestants needed to form alliances, cheat on one another, stab each other in the back, and so on. Now with something so obviously contrived, one may wonder how it was framed as authentic television (we will talk more about authenticity in the next section). Well, narrative transportation. Audiences knew the show was scripted, but they also saw it as authentic if they could connect with one of the characters or connect with the way a character acted in a certain situation (Rose and Wood 2005). If they could transport themselves into that narrative, they could keep the brand relationship going and therefore keep watching the series.

Let's return to Heath's work on low-attention processing. In his lectures to students, Heath uses the Flower Seller advertisement that helped build the Stella Artois brand in the United Kingdom. The situation presents a beautifully idealized scene of rural Belgium, involving simple humor, few words, and a flower seller trading his flowers with an inn keeper for a pint of Stella Artois beer. How does this work? There is no call to action or even attempt to persuade you of the brand's merits. And with beer, there is really very little actual difference between products, especially for mass market lager. As Heath tells it, and we are simplifying, the scene plays to UK consumers stereotypical image of the French countryside (it's Belgium but the music is very French to the ears of the consumer), and that signals romance, quality, and sensual appeal. Because the French are perceived to have a passion for food and drink, it must be really good, otherwise why would the seller trade all his beautiful flowers for it? It plays to consumers' expectations of iconic authenticity, or how things ought to be, and as a result it is attractive. The tagline 'Reassuringly expensive' (again, not a call to action) reinforces the impression made by the other associations. The result was mass-market penetration, until, and this really is why co-creation is a double-edged sword, the brand got associated with binge drinking and violence against women and became known as 'wife beater' in popular culture.

keeping it real? what is all the fuss about brand authenticity?

Not so long ago, in what does seem like a different galaxy, the idea that a brand could be authentic was sneered at. Brands were the opposite of authenticity. As cool places were gentrified by hipster brands, critics and residents decried the loss of authenticity. The slow food movement was started partly to counteract the loss of authentic local cuisines, ingredients, and traditions brought about by big fast-food chains (and their even larger industrial suppliers). One could even use prefixes such as Mc- or Coca- to refer to how authentic culture, work, or places were being lost.

However, marketers never miss an opportunity. The late comedian Bill Hicks who left one in no doubt about his anti-marketing views ('kill yourselves, seriously!') ironically argued that those who were turned off by marketing might be a great segment to actually tap into. Paradoxically, although Hicks was being cynical, he remains beloved by marketers (often of a certain age and gender) for his insights into what became known as the ironic hipster segment. This theme was taken further by marketer extraordinaire, foul-mouthed fourth-grader Eric Cartman (yes, he of *South Park* fame) who turned a failing theme park (renamed Cartmanland) into the hottest destination in town simply by declaring that no one was allowed to enter it. Brands may not fit the ancient Greek ideal of authenticity, but modern marketers have created so much authenticity in branding that it is now not only *passé*, but also measured as part of financial brand metrics. What happened?

In two words, luck and wine (the good stuff just to be clear). Many ideas are the result of serendipity, which can be assisted with stimulants, but in this case the wine came before the luck. The first author of the text had spent several years working in and around the wine industry and had even gained a PhD focused on firm development in the wine sector (well someone had to do it!). While teaching in France he got the idea for examining luxury brands after many of his brilliant students identified icons such as Chanel, Louis Vuitton, and so on as places they'd like to work. These brands seemed very old, and at least on the surface, did not fit standard textbook explanations for endurance. An idea was born.

Knowing little of luxury fashion and accessories, your author decided to start with wine, which he knew, and quickly submitted a grant proposal to go and visit some of France's greatest wine estates to collect data. You can imagine the looks on the faces of grant panel members – 'he wants money to go and chat over wine?!' they said. But here's where having some personal brand equity counts (you might call it connections but I'm sticking with personal brand equity) and one member noted that it was indeed a serious proposal and should be granted. Well, they grudgingly agreed, trimming the funding by a derisory amount just to remind your author who was boss and off to France he went. Before reading on, bear in mind the research was conducted in rural France during winter, so wine was needed for health reasons!

Your hard-working author went to some of the world's finest wine estates, talked to the owners, marketers, and estate managers (over wine), and was generally treated very very well. A little knowledge is often helpful and although the discussions had been informative, after some tours of the estates he began to suspect he was being told a set of myths, in a very a charming French way. The whole story was a bit more complicated. What he realized is that there was a front stage of branding that talked about craft, passion, beauty and a lack of commercial understanding, and a backstage of technological advancement, marketing expertise, and business acumen (Beverland 2005).

Both were essential for brand endurance, but why were they telling just one part of the story (at a time when the so-called old world, of which France was part, was being lambasted as stuck in mud, backward looking and worse, non-market oriented)? The answer was simple. These firms needed all the science and marketing expertise to continue to lead the world in perceived quality and therefore earn price premiums, but no one really wanted to know that. Every expert in the sector pretty much knew the reality of how these firms operated, but they wanted to believe the myths. And consumers were more than happy to play along.

Now that sounds like your author is rather brilliant, discovering ideas quickly. But to be honest, he was struggling with the data largely because the luxury angle was dull, and could not really get past the idea that he had been sold a set of myths albeit by people he felt were really genuine or sincere about what they were doing. This is where luck came in. He saw a call for papers in the *Journal of Management Studies* on understanding authenticity in organizations. That word was the angle he was looking for, and an article, 'Crafting Brand Authenticity: The Case of Luxury Wine', was born. Subsequently cited, it resulted in a series of papers that eventually bought the two authors of your guide together, which means we can return to using the editorial 'we',

Our initial idea was simple – a well-crafted story could generate a sense of authenticity for a brand, if it aligned with what consumers expected. Consumers would put aside (or more accurately, push aside) any objections as long as the story chimed with what they wanted to believe. Turns out others were also onto the same idea. Kent Grayson and Radan Martinec conducted a series of experiments for a seminal *Journal of Consumer Research* article in 2004. They tested how consumers reacted to a fictional but well-known theme site (The Sherlock Holmes Museum in London, which pretends to be Holmes' historic abode), and a real historic site (the birthplace of William Shakespeare, apparently a playwright of some note). They expected consumers would not only see the latter as more real, but also more desirable. They were to be sorely disappointed! Well, until they realized what they had really found. Consumers not only saw the stylistically real as genuine or authentic but preferred it over the objectively true site.

We've already discussed the case of serial brand *Survivor*, which was sold as 'reality television' (and which featured in a study by Rose and Wood (2005)). Your first author and his long-suffering colleague Francis Farrelly examined this further in their 2010 article 'The Quest for Authenticity in Consumption'. They found that consumer goals underpinned a process of authenticity judgments, and that consumers happily engaged in confirmation bias to generate their desired outcome. A brand such as McDonald's was seen as authentically local (in this case Australian) because it had been a long-time player in the community, raising funds via its Ronald McDonald House program, hosting children's birthdays, being the place where teenagers hung out and often got their first job, and so on. And, it had adapted its menu to include the much-loved *McOz* (which was basically a quarter pounder with a piece of beetroot added to it). Consumers motivated by a desire for community would put aside any ethical concerns over the brand's operations and find it to be a genuine authentic partner.

While this was going on, the 2008 global financial crisis hit (and was quickly rebranded as the GFC), impacting on local communities and forcing governments to bail out banking brands who had been behaving in ways even *No Logo* couldn't have predicted. The impact on branding was that consumers began to reconsider, at least for a moment, the impact on their communities of their purchase behavior. Older brands, with seemingly ye olde tyme values, such as Woolrich, Hellman's Mayo, Pendleton, and so on continued to produce locally, and therefore purchasing from them was seen as an investment in local jobs and local communities. A book on brand authenticity would seemingly be perfect for the times, which was exactly what the first author delivered.

Beverland's (2009) *Building Brand Authenticity: 7 Habits of Iconic Brands* (which fetches ridiculous prices on second-hand sites) broke down what it took to be authentic as a brand. The book found a willing audience with practitioners, especially advertising creatives, and led to major alcohol conglomerates running ads talking about their passion and their lack of concern for money (which should serve as a warning for aspiring business writers, be careful what you wish for), featuring their now-valued workforce, imagined local communities, and newly discovered long-held values. Subsequently quantitative research honed these ideas further, with authors demonstrating that authenticity did pay (Becker, Wiegand et al. 2019), and even major brand agencies adding authenticity measures into their valuation exercises.

So why do so many people get authenticity wrong? And why do some really get uptight and angry (and we mean really angry) about it? Well, both see authenticity as something that is actually true, not something that just feels right. Authenticity is what we call a market construct, it's socially agreed upon and therefore no matter how much heritage you may have, for example, if you don't conform to expectations of what authenticity should be, you'll be seen as fake. This is why saying your brand is authentic is a huge mistake – those that are don't need to say it, they show it. Similarly missing the point are the critics claiming that consumers' constant preferences for the seemingly fake make a mockery of authenticity.

Plenty of studies demonstrate this point, but since you expect us to conform to what academics should be, let's mention one of our own. Researchers on authenticity typically like to study particular categories of products, wine, craft beer, Champagne, chocolate, cheese, Tiki bars, and so on. You can probably spot the pattern even if we can't. Having got a little tired of luxury wine, your first author teamed up with some colleagues to study Belgian beers known as 'special beers' by connoisseurs. We examined the communications of authentic Trappist beers and those who sought to copy them, known at the time as 'abbey ales'. You can probably guess what happened. Consumers thought pretty much all were probably making things up, but once again, those bearing the authentic Trappist logo lost out to those that were crafted to fit with expectations about historic beers produced by monks.

Abbey ales used all sorts of tricks such as gothic fonts, stained glass imagery, religious iconography, and stylized images of monks to project a sense of timeless tradition. And it worked. When we studied the sector, we found that demand for these types of beers were growing, but because they were made in small batches by craftsman (i.e., monks), supply was not meeting demand. Big brewers though had no credibility in making these beers. So what did the big brewery groups do? True to form they first tried to buy the Trappist brands, but most of their representatives were cursed and some were burnt at the stake. So, they tried to look for monastic orders that no longer made beers, hence the term abbey ale. Failing that they tried to buy old abbeys and turn them into factories. At some point someone realized all of that was unnecessary, and even owning a few ruins was a folly. All they needed to do was look to part. The poor Trappists never knew what hit them (they're still around by the way, the category just expanded massively, and beer drinkers and big breweries benefitted) (Beverland et al. 2008).

Authenticity is always subjectively experienced; truth claims are possibly a hindrance more than a help. In fact, authors have noted how authenticity as truth is possibly the hardest claim to render in the market (Moulard 2021). So what is authenticity? Basically a sense of being true, genuine, and real. That's pretty vague and better authors have spent lots of thinking time, usually without visiting vineyards and breweries, distinguishing between authenticity as consistency (i.e., you do what you say you'll do), authenticity as conformity (you conform to communal norms), and authenticity as connection (like the beer example, some imagined connection to type, such as links to place, or in the beer case, religion) among many other schemes. What this means is authenticity can be rendered, scarily easily, and it seems to pay off. Since it's an enduring value, at least in the West, the desire for something real doesn't seem to be diminishing, and brand marketers are only too happy to help. So keep it real, by faking it well.

the logo-ism sinners were right all along

Until recently, you could probably be forgiven for thinking that the external signs of brands, such as logos, taglines, colors, fonts were unexciting. Some condemned any interest in communication devices as 'logo-ism', a phrase intended as an insult for naïve commentators on brands who equated said signs with the subtle art of branding itself. There is of course some logic to this view. While logos and all that are often derided by the person in the street as empty status-giving devices that force the weak into paying price premiums, they are of course the most visible and ubiquitous aspects of branding, strategically placed in communications and carefully displayed in movies and game tie-ins. Just watch post-match interviews with top tennis players as they carefully maneuvre their hands to ensure their brand-new luxury watch provided by a prominent sponsor of grand slam tournaments is placed within camera shot. (Curiously enough, the watch is nowhere in sight during the match, but is slipped casually on the wrist as soon as the match is over). While this generates some amusement (at least it does for us, but then again, we're easily amused), it also reflects the power of well-known logos to communicate brand origin and associations to the global audience watching online.

Since logos are everywhere, it's no wonder that many people equate them with the practice of branding per se. Not for nothing do many of us start a class or lecture on branding with a quick icebreaker that involves showing students nothing more than partial logos, fonts, color schemes, and if needed, some cryptic message about a brand to test students' knowledge. Unsurprisingly, brands with substantial power, such as Apple and Nike, generate instant recognition from most of the class, while others, such as specialist drink Jägermeister or the terminally dead Playboy, generate confused looks. A quick discussion often follows, in which students point out that the exercise is easy because brands are all around us, and that they remain unchanged, by which they mean the colors, fonts, styles, associations, and so on have been invested in for many decades.

Recently however, these mundane external signs of the brand have made a comeback, by being reframed as assets, or brand assets to be specific. The all-powerful Ehrenberg–Bass Institute is largely responsible, with Jenni Romaniuk's (2018) *Building Distinctive Brand Assets* converting many to the cause, with its discussion of asset fame and uniqueness. For converts to the brand asset cause, the focus is on strategically leveraging things such as forms, images, words, colors, and labels. Some of these build fame, which relates primarily to the category the brand competes in, while others build uniqueness. According to Romaniuk, the aim is to maximize fame and uniqueness for each asset. Failing that, consideration should be given to streamlining (i.e., reducing) assets for greater efficiency.

Despite this, many brand managers run hot and cold on their most unique asset, the logo. Logos are often changed, dropped, and messed with, usually generating an immediate backlash, which results in the original being revived with the brand claiming they had 'listened to consumers' (which arguably should have occurred before the change, not after). Some changes even cause angst on a national scale, such as the decision by Finland's most famous glassware brand Iittala to drop its distinctive exclamation mark in a red dot (the logoed sticker was often unremoved by owners and left to slowly fade through repeated washing), only to replace it what looks like an AI-generated luxury brand logo that is decidedly unlovable. Mess with logos that reflect national identity at your peril, would seem to be sage advice. Luxury brand managers go through cycles of logo-extremism, to logo-embarrassment, as they switch between a desire to emphasize conspicuous consumption and manage the backlash against it through inconspicuous, slow luxury (in which the uppity logo is put in its place, at least for a time).

Strangely, marketers rarely seem to mess with their other assets. Changing colors can be expensive, and even almost-dead Kodak still retains widespread awareness for its distinctive red and yellow K. Renaming exercises typically generate even more swearing by profanity-prone marketing journalists, with some as PwC's decision to rename themselves 'Monday' being permanently etched into branding's wall of shame. Few in their right mind would be tempted to add the word 'new' to their name to refresh their brand, lest they also want to be associated with one of marketing's greatest fails, the New Coke. Instead, the assets are tweaked, retouched, give greater or lesser prominence, stretched, extended, and protected.

Coincidentally (or concurrently), once written-off assets, particularly mascots, have returned with a vengeance. This is partly because they are easier to control than all-too-human (therefore fallible) spokespeople, are cheaper than famous people, and are efficient (no allowance needs to be made for different cultures or even inclusivity issues). Because they are often animal in their form, they also appeal to the child in all of us. Thus, while brands endanger the natural word, brand managers have been pillaging the animal kingdom (without paying royalties) presenting us with happy cows, chipper bulldogs, pandas, owls, tunas, meerkats, geckos, and tigers, all of which sadly may outlive their real-world referents who are in danger of going extinct.

Whether these are assets in the original sense of the word is debateable. Selling off logos without supporting patents or underlying physical infrastructure (such as premium vineyards that seem somewhat important to what goes in the premium label of a Champagne) may work in boom times, but those who manage to return previously dead brands to life (after buying said assets at fire-sale prices) are rare.

Brand marketers perhaps need to start being more at ease with their logos, names, taglines, and other brand assets. They have been bequeathed to them by their professional forbears, and are often loved or at least well-liked by consumers, retailers, and members of the public. But for goodness' sake, use professionals to generate and refresh them! Watching a few YouTube videos on how to design a great logo does not qualify you as a creative (spend more of your time honing the brief so creatives don't have to second-guess what you want).

chapter summary

If you'd paid attention, you will now be able to speak like a branding pro, and perhaps even have some useful prompts for your AI-generated strategy (let's not even pretend you'll write it yourself). These are just a few of the key considerations in brand marketing, but they are also some of the most important ones. We've covered issues of brand strategy, from positioning to extension and the management of portfolios of brands, through to more technical aspects of brand research and assessment, and even some overlooked issues surrounding implementation such as those involving employees and supportive systems. And, since your practice is simply performative you'll appreciate the advice on how to fake authenticity like a pro. So get going on your latest brand pitch or better yet, go and terrorize your marketing team with your newfound knowledge.

5

Enduring Challenges in Branding

who creates brand meaning?

We often run an in-class exercise where we ask students to identify all the associations a brand has. Harley Davidson is an old favorite so let's think about its generally accepted associations of rebellion, freedom, and masculinity. We know consumers see this brand as being something that enables them to be a rebel and escape the conformity of their weekly lives, but how did this occur? Well, the motorcycles were ridden by gangs like the Hell's Angels, modern-day bandits who reject society's rules. The motorcycle also featured in counter-culture movies such as *Easy Rider* which laments the decline of the traditional American male, and in which the protagonists ride off into the sunset (much like the lone riders did in Westerns of old). The Terminator (played by Arnold Schwarzenegger) rode one in the second instalment of that branded franchise which, incidentally, has the advantage of relying on time travel and therefore can always reboot its brand for new generations (although not terribly well).

So who creates brand meaning? In the case of Harley Davidson, over decades of brand decline it was consumers and popular culture that kept the associations alive. Since the 1990s Harley's brand marketers started to play a role in reinforcing these associations and adding new ones, but as Holt identifies, they represent just one author of the brand's meaning. Consumers are another, as is the way in which the brand is framed in popular culture. And we also have influencers, members of the press, associations of particular professions, and so on that help shape the meaning of the brand. Where Marty Neumeier may claim that no one else can tell you what a brand may mean to you, the reality is our image of a brand is shaped by many sources and in this sense, we now say brand meaning is co-created. This doesn't let wannabe brand managers off the hook, so don't get too comfortable, your job is about to get a whole lot harder.

Therefore, asking who creates brand meaning is somewhat misleading. We hope it's clear to you by now that there are multiple influences on brand meaning, and that what marketers intend for their brands is not always how others see them. So it's not so much who creates brand meaning, but what the implications are of multiple brand authors or influences on practice. This is where things get tricky. In 2004, Vargo and Lusch announced that marketing was now governed by a service-dominant logic, putting co-creation firmly at the heart of marketing. Put simply, service-dominant logic holds that consumers do not buy goods for materialistic reasons but for the services they provide. Brands therefore must appeal to what Clayton Christensen and colleagues (2016) called 'customers' jobs to be done' or JTBD, an acronym that is thrown around among marketing practitioners today, often with little understanding of what it truly means.

Jobs to be done actually encapsulate a whole range of insights about consumers, regardless of perspective. So for consumer culture theorists, identity motives, both individual and collective, are identity jobs. For the more behaviorally minded, the distinctiveness of the brand may appeal to a simpler, more functional job, and so on. Although Christensen et al.'s focus was always innovation, the application of JTBD to marketing and branding makes sense and, if understood broadly, is extremely useful. The problem is that too many marketers look at the term 'job' and assume it must be a practical need, which leads them to focus on functional benefits (you may argue this makes sense in terms of an innovation-focused framework, which would be a fair assessment, but nevertheless flawed as a way of framing consumer needs). Like Fournier's emphasis on knowing the consumer and the world they inhabit, JTBD requires you to do the same, and, critically, also acknowledges consumers' role as active meaning creators with whom you must co-create solutions (and yes, whether you are selling goods or services, consumers are buying only the latter).

So what does co-creation involve? The service-dominant logic was in effect relationship marketing 2.0 for many academics and was always framed as a paradigm shift in marketing. Paradigm shifts are always good for keeping one mentally nimble, but they can also lead to cult-like devotion by some, as we found out when we met our academic nemesis, Reviewer 2 (and to be fair, reviewers 1 and 3) during an article revision. Said article demonstrated that brand managers' embrace of co-creation often led them focus more on sustaining consumers' desired brand narratives through practices that may seem at first glance, duplicitous. This was met with wholesale rejection on the basis that unless one involved consumers directly in the brand identity process, no co-creation was occurring. We like to think we won the argument eventually, as one of the many rewrites of service-dominant logic's foundational principles clearly state that co-creation of meaning does not require direct input from consumers (Merz et al. 2009). (The other thing about paradigms is they are self-generative of the need for updates, which are great for academic careers.) We may have won the argument, but of course, the article languishes somewhere in digital purgatory, having never seen the light of day.

Christensen and friends argue that JTBD are often discovered by looking at consumer practices. People often cannot articulate what they really need but can give you an insight into their lived experiences, or talk to you about things they dislike, avoid, or develop workarounds for. All of these are opportunities for innovations that make it easier for consumers to do their jobs, often by removing so-called 'pains' and addressing 'gains' (we never can escape the logic of utility maximization from economics, it seems). Platform brands, for example, are positioned on this basis. Often framed in terms of access-on-demand, these brands claim to help consumers overcome the inefficiency of owning stuff on an as-needs basis. While their claims do speak to consumer needs, the brands rarely sat down with consumers (or indeed critical stakeholders such as local councils and so on), as they were largely technology-driven.

Consumers not being able to fully articulate their needs doesn't necessarily mean engaging with them in the co-creation of meaning is a bad idea. That said, as the 2017 competition to name the National Oceanographic Centre's flagship research vessel showed, giving consumers full rein will likely end up in disaster (if it had been up to the public vote, the good ship would have been named Boaty McBoatface). Not that marketers are much better – in 2009, despite having plenty of good naming ideas for a brand extension of Australian icon brand *Vegemite*, the team at Kraft still decided to go with *iSnack 2.0*. To give credit where it's due, the team were quick to do a *mea culpa* and let consumers decide on the more effective Cheesy Bite (the new product was a blend of cream cheese and *Vegemite*, showing once again that there really is no accounting for taste).

A critical issue in the co-creation of brand meaning is the terms of engagement. For example, allowing consumers' input into collabs, names, product decisions, and other more tactical aspects that are part of keeping the brand fresh is common for a social media influencer, although the choices are usually controlled by the person-brand's team. This type of co-creation leads to engagement among followers and strengthens the bonds they have with the brand and within their community. Brand managers may also engage in similar strategies. Returning to *Vegemite*, the brand team decided to ask Aussies how they loved their *Vegemite* as a means of generating conversations about the brand, which at the time was in decline. This created a wave of consumer-generated content that stimulated new uses and shifted the brand away from is waning associations with breakfast and the predominantly white 1970s Australia.

Although writers on cultural branding tend to stress the brilliance of the creative teams behind the campaigns that reinvigorate icons (opening themselves up to charges of leaving little room for the consumer as meaning-maker), in practice much work is done behind the scenes to understand consumer identity struggles. This type of work may be ethnographic in nature, whether conducted in the real or digital space (this distinction is fairly meaningless in this day and age, but we still feel obliged to say it to avoid annoying those on either side of the digital divide) or involve depth interviews that often utilize tools that became associated with 'design thinking', which in reality just meant what designers did (and how).

Design thinking became all the rage around 2008 when Tim Brown of IDEO popularized the idea that everyone could, and indeed should, become a designer. Unfortunately this tended to mean questionable fashion choices and a love of Post-it Notes in strategy sessions. But many of the tools are useful for co-creating meaning. We use these in class when discussing the teaching case of IDEO helping a Peruvian cinema chain renew itself to see off the threat of streaming brands such as Netflix. The central exercise asks a regular cinema goer to diarise their average week. Within this discussion, the brand team begins to realize that this consumer is immensely time poor, as he works, studies, and maintains relations with his parents. The insights gained from this exercise make the team realize that going to cinema for this consumer is a mix of jobs to be done, including the desire for escape and to reaffirm his status as eldest son with his beloved parents. Within this discussion the team realizes that central to enhancing the consumer's journey is the removal of any pain points that add time and stress, while investing in gain creators that give the consumer more control over his entertainment experience with his family (Buell and Otazo 2016).

Regardless of any association with what might be a management fad, the tools used by the creative disciplines are often focused on discovery or exploration, and attempt to get an understanding of the messiness of the consumer world that Fournier identified was so central to understanding a consumer's brand relationship. Ultimately, these tools try to uncover latent needs, or needs consumers may not realize they consciously have, but nonetheless represent potential solutions to frustrating jobs to be done. Other techniques that brands use to get at this lived experience often include communal brand strategies and ensuring staff involvement in the focal activities of the brand. Nike, for example, require staff to be involved in sport in some way so that they can gain an array of insights from the field, including individual consumer experiences, beliefs about product performance, and the culture and rituals of particular teams or sports. All of these provide insights that can make the brand speak with the cultural authority necessary for authenticity.

Co-creation also occurs when brand managers offer solutions to identity crises that consumers may experience. This is particularly important for brands that may embody collective identity markers such as femininity, masculinity, the shared myths underpinning national identity, and other market constructs such as success, morality, authenticity, cool, and so on. One way to do this is to track conversations via sentiment analysis and other computer-based tools to identify shifting conversations and even imagery on these core issues. For example, in many Western economies the idea that young people will be better off than their parents has started to diminish, with concerns raised about the ability to access the housing market (in the 2000s), afford children, and even enjoy job security. For brands that position themselves as aspirational or even those that suggest they are a reward for hard work, how would this trend effect their ability to solve a consumer's JTBD?

Helen Edwards (2023) suggests brands themselves should play a role in mainstreaming marginal practices or ideas, not only as a form of innovation, but as a way of enabling consumers to achieve their identity goals. She built up a significant database of marginal behaviors such as eating insects and micro-dosing with narcotics, examined what it would take to mainstream some of these, and provided a range of indicators to identify the potential for shifts in marginal behaviors as a means of co-creating value. The most recent example of mainstreaming would be the rapid shift in fortunes around veganism. While there have been so-called vegans since the term was developed in the 1944 by the Vegetarian Society in the United Kingdom, the practice remained marginal for many decades despite published health benefits, debates about animal-related ethics and even demonstrations of enhanced sustainability. The problem was the image mainstream consumers had of vegans and veganism was not appealing. Brands played a role in reframing this practice as plant-based and enabled non-vegans to change their behaviors slowly, which helped them address concerns around diet and sustainability and even ethics.

art and science, the challenge of scientific laws vs. the creative genius

The age-old question – is marketing, and by implication branding, an art or a science? No doubt you will guess we'd say it's both and you'd be right. The question remains important and enduring. At the time of writing we'd say that the science aspect of branding is in the ascendency, or at least for those claiming to offer a scientific approach to branding. The qualification we add is important because those claiming to offer truths often base their views on a very narrow and arguably self-serving view of science. The broad base of academic and practitioner brand knowledge draws on many traditions and methods, the best of which meets the highest standards of accepted rigor within their fields. Science therefore is not simply the domain of one group, usually reserving the title of law-like generalizations for their own research findings.

The art vs. science debate in branding takes many forms, and while we sit somewhere in the middle of this, an understanding of the recent history of brand management gives us the confidence to say that this debate is worthwhile. Why? Largely because each period in which one side or the other dominates does result in breakthroughs and useful ideas. Each period also often balances out the previous one, moving practitioners away from extremes, which often generates better branding. And, the two sides also interact, with those in favor of science often highlighting the importance of creativity while denigrating what they see as poorly defined constructs or claims, while those advocating art often generating a large array of creative approaches to branding, which allow the field to innovate.

This interplay is important as it tends to reflect how new approaches become accepted knowledge within a field. Studies of knowledge development, for example, identify how a new idea often generates a large number of exploratory studies and tentative claims, while at the same suffering from definitional fragmentation and a lack of measurement. Eventually, if such ideas are to become more widely accepted as knowledge, definitions are agreed, measures developed, and relationships between variables examined (Hirsch and Levin 1999). For example, the idea of brand authenticity developed in this way. Authors (including us) generated a range of studies exploring the idea of authenticity in different product categories. We offered insights into the nature of authenticity and its role in brand relationships. But the array of contexts and approaches led to a multitude of definitions and in some cases, rather circular ones. Subsequently, authors integrated all this literature to generate some accepted definitions, developed scales of authenticity, and undertook experiments to understand causal inferences (Lehman et al. 2019; Morhart et al. 2015). The results helped provide insights into new ways to generate brand equity, among many other things.

In contrast, one could argue that something such as brand purpose has yet (at the time of writing) to move beyond the exploratory phase. As such, given the loss of confidence among practitioners in the value of such an idea, brand purpose may be in danger of premature death. Definitional challenges abound with some arguing purpose is what the brand offers for society, a higher order set of values, or alignment with social causes, while others use it interchangeably with brand activism (a more tactical approach which we think may offer greater value). On top of that it's difficult to distinguish brand purpose from an organization's mission, or corporate social responsibility. Then there's the wildly conflicting outcomes and a lack of attention to measurement. We may regret writing this, but we suspect brand purpose will not pass the rigor test and become accepted as scientific knowledge.

With this process established, hopefully you can see both the value of the art vs. science debate and the danger of favoring one side over the other. This debate over the decades has taken many forms. Scientific advertising, for example, was a view in the 1970s that was a precursor to the marketing performance approach today. Whereas historically, advertising for brands was attributed solely to great creative (which was an extremely narrow reading of how giants such as David Ogilvy viewed advertising), scientific advertising could demonstrate a link to sales outcomes. The problem was, this tended to favor an emphasis solely on functional benefits coupled with price promotion. In the short term these are effective, but as subsequent studies by marketing scientists such as John Philip Jones (1998) demonstrated, promotions can destroy brand equity as they diminish the image of the brand in the eyes of consumers. A more scientific approach argued for an emphasis on benefits contained within great creative, and for price promotions to occur within brand-driven advertisements.

A similar approach is playing out at present, with an emphasis on social media promotions. These again have the advantage of being able to demonstrate almost immediate results in terms of sales, but the same danger for the brand's image applies. The solution to this is for brand managers to acknowledge the need for advertising to have both a short- and long-term brand effect, and that promotions must therefore be handled with care (Jones 1998). Those advocating short-term effects have persuasive power with senior managers because they can demonstrate the financial effectiveness of their promotions. Historically, marketers have shied away from setting financial targets in favor of softer measures such as engagement, satisfaction, likeability, and likelihood to buy. But there is no excuse for any of this today and the true branding scientist will be an advocate for the power of creative, short-term activations that trigger outcomes and campaigns that help build long-term brand image. Failing brand managers will continue to sit disgruntled in the back of board meetings (assuming they're invited), bemoaning the lack of 'strategy' or an emphasis on instrumental results over creative genius.

However, one must also be careful of those claiming to be holders of the sole truth in branding. We are reminded of critiques of various movements claiming to be scientific, but in fact being rather cult-like in their approach. One such movement included the objectivism movement (or followers of the late Ayn Rand) who stress the centrality of reason, rationality, and objective truth. The critique is that science is always open to potential revision, never truly settled in that sense, and defined by a skeptical approach to truth claims (which must be subject to a process of falsification).

While advocates of scientific branding laws such as Ehrenberg–Bass have much to offer (we really do mean this, the challenge to the value of loyalty was long time coming), their adherents often seem too ready to dismiss any critique, embrace any finding unquestionably, and often are rather silent on their assumptions. Furthermore, studies contradicting their results are all too often dismissed in *ad hominem* style attacks, such as Sharp's (2010) dismissal of consumer psychology because of a few high-profile frauds within the field (whose work is typically retracted). While poor behavior exists in every field, every year there are hundreds of carefully conducted, rigorous studies undertaken by consumer psychologists who increasingly provide full access to their data to allow for replication and checking. Greater openness to alternate approaches and even seemingly contradictory findings are hallmarks of science and are essential for advancing our knowledge of branding.

relevance and consistency: how to remain forever new, without changing

Many of the things we have discussed so far involve breathing life into your brand position, largely by ensuring it is consistently delivered. Consistency is of course a good thing, both in life, and critically, in branding. Brands are a promise to the consumer, and despite claims that being a trickster brand archetype allows you to mess things up every now and again, it often leaves customers wondering if the brand is just taking the piss. Being consistent helps build points of distinction, and critically, has been demonstrated to drive brand equity.

But much like a band who keeps to a formula, eventually we can tire of more of the same. New acts seem fresher, our tastes change, and as Ehrenberg–Bass reminds us, loyalty is a leaky bucket, requiring us always to top up our customer base with new users. Placing a premium on consistency also locks us into reproducing the same ideas and associations, often in the same way, despite diminishing returns and falling relevance. Further, a preference for consistency may blind brand managers to possibilities that can enable growth or, at the very least, retain existing customers, particularly those such as retailers who are often the conduits for relevance within particular categories.

No doubt this all sounds reasonable, but those of you still following (or at least are awake) may notice a problem. How does one balance the need to be consistent with the need to be relevant? It's a version of the age-old problem in strategy of stability and change. Brands build up points of distinction in the eyes of consumers over time, and as you should appreciate at this stage, these matter. Regardless of your position on the value of loyalty, everyone largely agrees that stable associations matter (even Douglas Holt holds that during periods of social stability, consistency is key) when it comes to building brand equity. However, everyone also agrees that change is needed to remain relevant, which is also an essential driver of brand equity. So how do we balance the two?

Historically the answer was to split them along strategic and tactical lines. Since it was the brand's position that must endure forever, strategically this should remain consistent over time. However, the tactics that reinforce this position, including the famous marketing mix, should always change. This was relatively easy for marketers to manage, since relevance involved decisions on new products, promotions, in-store displays, aspects of communications, and so on, all of which were simply aimed at remaining fresh. Since these were all guided by the unchanging brand position, marketers could comfort themselves that they were being consistent while also changing.

You may be tempted to ask, why the somewhat cynical tone in all of this? Well, marketers are well-trained in the logic of brand reinforcement, leading them to frame every decision around the brand in a way that privileges staying 'on-brand', regardless of whether it makes sense to do so. Holt characterizes this as a brand bureaucracy which ultimately becomes a brand straitjacket that provides a sense of control and no room for movement (admittedly an apt metaphor, since the constant desire to always be on-brand may result in senior managers shouting 'nurse!' more than once). We view this somewhat more sympathetically in that marketers, much like any discipline, view the world through a particular cognitive frame, which provides useful but incomplete insights. Most of the time, consistency is the answer, and freshening up the mix to appeal to all potential consumers does work. It's just sometimes, more radical change is needed, and also, one can broaden the position of the brand without necessarily diluting its essential character.

Academic brand researchers too suffer from a cognitive frame, which strangely excludes a focus on understanding the challenges faced by brand managers in dealing with strategic challenges (beyond recounting the anecdotes we all know and love). Therefore, we know that consumers like new content to be presented in familiar ways and that seemingly off-brand extensions need to be tied back to some aspect of the brand's perceived heritage, but less about how brand managers balance the different logics involved in consistency and relevance over time. Two exceptions to this are studies on cultural branding and brand ambidexterity.

Cultural branding starts from a position that largely privileges change. Rooted in Fournier's work on brand relationships and other identity-driven studies that do not privilege the manager's view of the brand, cultural branding identifies that when the consumer and/or something in their wider world from which they draw identity changes, then the brand's historic position is largely worthless as a resource. This leads to an understanding of the limits of brand management models that are based on an emphasis on consistency, and also explores the nature of strategy making that enables change.

Some, such as Holt and Giesler, simply argue one should discard the historic position and move to something more relevant. Others suggest viewing the brand formula as a set of building blocks that themselves can be mashed up and reformulated in ways that are recognizably of the brand, but also reflect changes in sector/category and/or societal practices. Who is right? Well, each answer tends to reflect the nature of the brand examined. The latter view reflects the management of serial brands, such as the 007 James Bond franchise, whose points of distinction are essential to the mythology of the brand, while the nature of category (entertainment) means updates are always essential to resonate with new audiences. Giesler's (2012) study of Botox in its growth phase highlights the emergent nature of brand position in a new category or technology, where growth is often given greater weight than loyalty. Holt's examination of challenger brands unsurprisingly emphasizes cultural innovation and change, while his work on more established brands gives rise to concerns about the ability of brand managers to innovate in terms of meaning without some outside help (usually from a new advertising agency).

An alternate approach was to examine the ways in which brand managers could manage across both demands at once. A study involving your first author identified the value of brand ambidexterity, or the capabilities marketers needed to manage change and stability over time. Ambidexterity has its roots in innovation and focuses on the ways in which firms can both exploit capabilities and or explore new possibilities. Etymologically the term refers to the ability to use both hands equally well, which may bestow unique advantages, as anyone who has watched snooker genius and person-brand Ronnie 'The Rocket'

O'Sullivan switching effortlessly from right to left hand because the success of the shot demands it (or because he simply feels like it). Although ambidextrous people and organizations may have a preference for right/left or exploitation/exploration, they have the ability to use both well when needed, which gives them an edge. So too with brands.

In their study of brand ambidexterity, Beverland et al. (2015) looked at a range of branding challenges where consistency was a barrier to value creation. These not only included the traditional challenge of relevance, but also instances where salespeople or retail clients were asking for product styles offered by competitors that were popular with consumers at the time, as well as desires to simply move into new markets. These latter challenges are more about exploring new possibilities for the brand, and therefore can either open up new pathways to growth, or sometimes just keep key stakeholders such as retailers happy (i.e., reinforce channel equity). But, at first glance, they seem decidedly off-brand, and hence must somehow be made on-brand to ensure internal support and external success. How?

The authors identified that a more disruptive problem-solving approach, similar to design thinking, was necessary. This involved using things like abductive reasoning, which has a 'what could be?' logic, that helps trigger creative problem-solving without dropping away key considerations like consistency. The focus went much more on understanding the why of the problem, rather than rushing to a solution. This problem focus often helps one contextualize market meanings, and therefore understand how to shift them. The authors identified a three-step process (of course they did, reviewers go mad for a three-step), starting with disruptive questioning, then the creation of the innovation, then transformation of the brand's narrative, which ensured relevance was balanced with consistency, but with a twist.

For example, the Diesel brand had built its reputation by innovating heavily in the denim category, playing to a younger audience with both sexually suggestive advertising and also messages that recognized and even encouraged those times when teenagers did stupid things. They could charge more than other brands of denim and believe us, they did. But they also faced an image problem. Eventually those silly teens grew up, got jobs, and became concerned about being seen as professional and adult (while it seems adults never stop trying to find their inner child). A brand based around casual wear, sexual profligacy, and stupidity was not going to cut it with former loyalists who were now working in investment banking (the rebels always sell out, after all you always have to feed the monkey). How could the brand keep these clients without ruining their image with a new generation of teenagers for whom their older siblings were decidedly uncool?

They invented a new brand called Diesel Labs. The use of the term 'lab' is one way of signaling experimentation. Diesel Labs was sold on the basis of being a luxury brand. The team was sourced from the fashion design elite, instructed to use any material but denim, allowed to price accordingly, and not held accountable for profits (which was fortunate). The lab quickly gained a reputation for inventiveness and luxury, which appealed heavily to older consumers keen to retain their own sense of style while fitting in with corporate dress codes and the strictures of snooty nightclubs (Grigorian and Chandon 2010). People started to see Diesel as a more than stupid sex-crazed kids in denim, which was all that was needed for head office to shut the lab and fold its design ethos into the parent brand. Diesel was still young, dumb, and denim, but also luxury, effortlessly stylish, and sophisticated. The brand was the same, but better.

All of these studies also alert us to the supportive environment necessary for managing this enduring brand challenge. While you may be tempted to think that in the case of serial brands, the creative context will allow ambidexterity to occur, we should not forget that brand-revitalizing films like *Casino Royale* are essential to recover from the critical dross of *Die Another Day* (plus the diminishing returns leading up to it). Not for nothing do we have the phrase 'jumping the shark' to refer to the point at which a serial brand started to decline in quality largely because the creative team had run out of ideas. Ambidexterity thrives when organizations allow for both consistency and relevance, which means they rely on more than one research tool, examine loyal and non-loyal audiences, keep an eye on the cultural fringe or margins to pick up on new social trends that may drive change, and support such risk-taking in their policies. They also renew their brand teams with new talent but then pair them up with more experienced members with the brief to allow mutual exchange of ideas.

Relevance used to be the poor cousin of consistency, but greater demands for growth, the realization that loyalty is less valuable than previously thought, and the power of social media to generate at the very least a temporal concern with particular issues that can impact on brand image have led to more respect for relevance. New metrics, such as Prophet's Brand Relevance Index have highlighted the alignment between customer centricity and relevance that, when coupled with brand authenticity, drive a sense of brand momentum or power. Balancing these two competing requirements necessitates managing different approaches to problem-solving and data collection, and a supportive environment for risk taking, rather than simply appointing a new agency, self-styled brand guru, or changing the logo.

can a brand change?

There's a scene in TV drama *The Wire*, where philosophical drug dealer Stringer Bell (played by Idris Elba) poses a problem for his economics lecturer. The professor is discussing the importance of price–quality trade-offs, identifying how one either needs to compete via price leadership or higher quality. Unfortunately for Bell, he has a problem that cannot be solved with either. He can't lower the price of the drugs he sells against a low-cost new entrant in his territory, nor can he compete on quality (let's just say his cocaine has been cut with numerous household products, dare we say invisible brands, and is unlikely to provide much of a hit). He asks the professor what he can do. The professor thinks for a minute and then smiles, 'I have a colleague in marketing who says in that situation, the only thing you can try is a rebrand'. For Bell, the rebrand didn't really work and since failure in this line of business is permanent, Elba didn't stick around after Season 3 (probably for the best too as the serial brand's quality also fell sharply afterwards, largely due to atrocious brand management).

Can you really change a brand? The answer is 'it depends', and often comes down to language and also the extent of damage done. Many marketers often talk about repositioning the brand when referring to brands that are in need some love. Usually these brands have declined over time, often through lack of attention to points of parity, a lack of innovation (including through extension), and internal neglect. But the term 'repositioning' is problematic. Jack Trout who co-authored branding classic *Positioning: The Battle for Your Mind*, subsequently wrote a follow up entitled *Repositioning: Marketing in an Era of Competition, Change and Crisis* (with Steve Rivkin) (2009). We can save you the trouble of seeking it out because the basic point stated very early on is 'you can't' or 'you shouldn't bother'. Why? Well think about the logic of positioning a brand. Positioning is in effect the brand's identity or point of distinctiveness, and if a brand has been successful at some point, consumers will know this is what the brand stands for. Repositioning is not the same as changing the brand's marketing mix and investing in some relevance-related actions. Rather, repositioning attempts to trick the consumer into believing the brand they once knew is now something entirely different. Trout argues that if positioning is to be believed, repositioning is not really possible or worth the effort. The dying brand is best harvested, sold to some other sucker – sorry, prudent investor – to milk for some cash flow for a while.

But is Trout just being too negative? There remain relatively few instances of brands really changing their position altogether. Maybe person-brands offer the best chance of this strategy as they can always argue they have matured or moved on from the past, but even there, how many examples spring to mind? Action movie stars rarely become serious dramatic actors, although comedians sometimes do. Disco pin-up John Travolta was repositioned as a more serious talent courtesy of Quentin Tarantino in *Pulp Fiction* (although Travolta subsequently starred in ultra-bomb *Battlefield Earth*, which didn't help his cause), but arguably stars that are rebooted by directors are often chosen because they've been written off and forgotten. They are literally used to reinforce the brands of directors such as Tarantino or the Coen Brothers, all of whom appeal to cinephiles who love such ironic casting choices.

While several brands have changed their name as a way of signaling a different intent, but often quickly return to their original. PricewaterhouseCoopers Consulting change to 'Monday' in 2002 is one infamous example (its owner IBM quickly scrapped the name). However, sometimes a name change is forced upon you. In 2020, the business school at City University in London was forced to drop its name, Cass, due to its associations with the 19th-century transatlantic slave trade. The John Cass foundation had already dropped the name of its benefactor, giving the business school little wriggle room (other business schools named after slavers had defended keeping their names), especially in the middle of the #blacklivesmatter protests following the killing of George Floyd by a US police officer. Herein lies the problem of being named after people – they either have a less-than-savory past (Cass was a particularly enthusiastic slaver) and if they are still around, they can go off and do silly things. After a thorough review, the business school was renamed Bayes Business School after the famous Bayes theorem devised by, you guessed it, (Thomas) Bayes. However, the school often still has to add 'formerly Cass' after their new name in publications and rankings in an effort to retain levels of awareness (Wiertz and Korschun 2021).

Not everyone agrees with Trout's rather negative view of the value of repositioning. Cultural brand authority Douglas Holt argues that brand position per se is not worth reifying and urges brand managers to change when the need arises. He is not saying, as others like Keller do, that one must simply freshen up the brand's marketing mix to ensure the position remains relevant. Holt actually cares little for notions of positioning. His view is that if there are wider changes in the culture that render your position irrelevant in the eyes of your consumers, then you must actually change. In his view, consumers really are nonplussed about your position. As long as you help them reflect their identity in ways that enable them to fit in, then you can be whatever the hell you want to be.

One example of this is serial brand, James Bond 007. One of the most successful franchise brands of all time, Ian Fleming's creation has remained relevant despite the decline of the United Kingdom as a world power, and changes in gender relations, social attitudes, race relations, audience expectations, and so on. But how? According to two academics who studied the brand over time (those like us who don't care for Bond can only imagine how these authors suffered for their work), the brand team mess with the core brand elements (actor, gadgets, villains, romantic relations, love of martinis, and so on) to reflect shifts in the industry environment and also the wider social environment (Preece et al. 2019). If you compare two Bonds, that of Timothy Dalton (much closer to Fleming's original characterization) and Pierce Brosnan, you can see why the former was wrong for the late 1980s while the latter was perfect for the early 1990s. Dalton played Bond as a cold, calculating killer, much as he was portrayed in the book. He was vengeful and downright nasty. But audiences at the time loved wise-cracking action heroes like Arnold Schwarzenegger and were not taken with Dalton's Bond. Brosnan was a perfect fit with the early 1990s emphasis on having a good time, but by the end of the decade, with new heroes such as Jason Bourne (another cold, calculating killer doubtful of the morality of his actions), he was passé, and more closely resembled Mike Myers' spoof secret agent Austin Powers. Actually, Dalton may have been perfect from the mid-1990s onwards, but when the time came to change, a younger actor was chosen. So brands remain relevant by shifting with the times. But did Bond really change that much, or even become something radically different?

Whether brands can escape their past is really the challenge. For social media influencer brands it's probably difficult because what happens online stays online, so it's always easy to trawl up old posts. But for tired brands, the ability to reposition often depends on how much time has passed between the brand's heyday and the repositioning. Take venerable film brand Kodak, which really was the Apple or Tesla of the 20th century. Awareness of the brand's assets remains high, as do its association with photographic film, which is a growing niche due to an analog revival, but not one with enough potential to excite the brand's investors. The brand had tried to reposition around commercial printing, stressing its heritage of vibrant color and quality but this market was very much a red ocean as they say, not one for the faint-hearted or the short of resources (and Kodak was nearing bankruptcy at the time).

But could they leverage their film heritage with new consumers? They certainly tried, focusing on making the brand cool with teens through licensed tie-ins with defunct fast fashion brands such as Forever 21 (as a sidenote, never use 'forever' in your brand name, it will always end in tears). This strategy was aimed at changing how people saw the brand and would provide a pathway for a slew of innovations. The only problem was those innovations didn't set the world alight and it was actually old-fashioned film that kept the brand going. But the attempt reflects how one might try and revive or rebrand, by going back into the brand's past and attempting to find a defendable point of authentic distinctiveness that might be relevant for a new audience.

Yamaha Music is one such example where they have rebranded through taking the connection a musician and audience has with music, and placing that, rather than technical expertise, at the heart of their brand. Undertaking some research that asked young consumers to draw Yamaha as a person, they found that their image was one of seriousness – the brand was an older man, single, never smiling, but very dedicated to his work. Not exactly what you'd expect for a brand that provided musical instruments for musicians of all abilities and genres across the globe. The problem was their image was missing the emotional connection that people had with music, focusing instead on the product features of their latest release. So the team rebranded Yamaha through the idea of 'Make Waves' which they believed captured the intention of a musician, the impact of the music, and connected to the wave form in music. After some best-in-class internal branding within a very skeptical and diversified corporation, the brand's own tracking suggested consumers were happy to follow along.

Perhaps the real problem comes down to how marketers misuse concepts such as repositioning, which is extremely difficult, to refer to things that are actually achievable, such as relaunching and refreshing. Yamaha was essentially a relaunch as the brand team took control of the entire visual look and feel of the brand for the first time. The brand's products had not changed, they simply decided to take things they could defend, that were relevant to their desired audience, and communicate them consistently through all channels. Relaunches can have different degrees. Some brands are literally brought back from the dead, such as luxury brand Emilio Pucci which was acquired by LVMH after lying dormant for many years. Here, repositioning is easier because there is simply less knowledge about the brand and one can therefore almost start with a clean slate, while leveraging connections with industry insiders such as the fashion press who will want to see the brand return to its glory. The longer the brand has been out of action, the more scope you have to do as you please.

Other changes are smaller, and often involve what we call a 'refresh'. This simply involves renewing associations, possibly by using more current spokespeople, or through new products and services, or a new campaign, and so on. These changes are often points of parity and largely should be part of the day-to-day proactive management of brands, so that equity continues to grow or at least doesn't decline in the face of change within society, among consumers, and competitors. We covered this in the section on stability and change earlier.

Change is one of those enduring challenges for brands. Here, we focus on the misuse of language around more substantive changes to brands brought on usually by declines in equity, or in rarer cases, environmental shocks or decisions for dramatic repositions (the shift from Twitter to X, is one such example that left many experts and indeed shareholders scratching their heads as to why). The jury is out on the possibility of true repositioning as the consumer brand image may hamper efforts to radically shift. However, different ways of framing consumer–brand relationships shape one's perspective on this issue. Furthermore, being clear about what degree of change one is talking about is important – so when you hear someone argue it's time to reposition, perhaps ask for clarification over why, and to what extent change is envisaged.

i want to live forever!

Brand managers of course hope their creations will be timeless. Advocates of authentic branding, such as yours truly, demand it (actually we say, 'appear timeless', there's a subtle difference lost on many). But is there a point at which you should end the brand's life? Why might they die? And do they stay dead, linger as ghost brands, or return from the grave, to haunt, sorry, enchant us once again? Can we cast spells to raise them from the dead?

Let's start with why brands die. Basically they get ill, can't be cured, and die. Brands can be abused substantially and often are, through neglect, or dilution (often through licensing agreements designed to provide much-needed funds for a failing business), but at some point, their equity falls to nothing. At this point, the brand per se, all its logos and promises, make no difference to anyone or anything.

There's a simple way to think about brand equity: how much would you pay for an item with a brand on it vs. the item without? If it's nothing, then the brand is ripe for end-of-life termination. Probably the last people to make the decision to terminate a brand will be brand managers. There is an unfounded belief that brands can forever be revived. Even some luxury car brands have often struggled for profit throughout their lives. Yet, to paraphrase chess grandmaster and marketing super (but not evil) genius Roland Rust (Rust et al. 2004), why do so many marketers not recognize the obvious, that failing brands are delivering no value? Being focused on value, Rust's view is brands that fail are consuming resources that could be better used elsewhere to deliver things customers actually want. But it's a brave brand manager who pulls the plug on a long-lived brand (who, other than Paul Atriedes in Frank Herbert's *Dune*, wants to go down in history as 'the one'?).

Fortunately there is a solution. There will always be someone more optimistic (or deluded, depending on how you want to look at it) about the potential of a failing brand than you. So you sell off its assets at (probably far) more than they're really worth and let someone else lose some money. We call this harvesting the brand, and it sounds so much nicer (after all, many of our holidays are harvest festivals). Brand managers used to love to gloat about the enormous size of their portfolios (as you can imagine, most of these brand managers were male). Having lots of brands made you stronger. Unfortunately, the finance folks spoiled the party as they are want to do and pointed out that competitors with just one brand also seemed to do pretty well, if not better than those with multiples. Some basic analysis showed that most of the brands in the portfolio underperformed, prompting many of the big brand conglomerates such as Unilever to regularly rationalize brand lines through harvesting. The result is more resources to put behind a few big brands and money to invest in growth categories and markets. Sometimes size is everything in branding (such as share of search and voice), but when it comes to portfolios, it's better to curate a smaller selection of brands that enjoy high growth or have the potential to do so.

The brands that die a slow death usually do so because of neglect. Sometimes they're just forgotten, as with New Zealand's premium beer Steinlager (which sounds suspiciously German, although that's where any connection with a good beer ends), which was 'simply forgotten' by the marketing team at Lion Nathan. Fortunately (we guess), the beer was revived, with a new bottle design, and for some reason seems to be doing well, prompting us to wonder if many other similarly terrible beers from the 1980s can be sold to cashed-up hipsters.

However, some brands suffer a quicker death, often because of toxic shock. These brands are those that fail spectacularly and are irredeemable in the eyes of key stakeholders. These are not just airlines that suffer crashes, but low-budget carriers like the ill-fated AirTran that crashed because they take shortcuts on safety. These are not just shock jocks (Australian slang for aggressive radio show hosts) that make the odd off-colored remark, they're ones who, after threatening to throttle then NZ Prime Minister Jacinda Ardern, find that no advertiser wants to be associated with the show. Mark Ritson refers to these brands as having negative brand equity, which is different from low brand equity. Negative brand equity is when the brand itself is so toxic that it is actually a turn-off (think Kevin Costner after *Waterworld* and *The Postman*). For these brands, death is the only answer.

are brands cultural parasites?

The heading may seem provocative, but it is essentially the charge levelled against brands in Douglas Holt's 2002 article with the ominous title 'Why brands cause trouble'. Rest assured this is not a rant against brands per se, but more an assessment of how brand managers often relate to the cultural world, on which some or much of their associations depend. As cultural anthropologist Grant McCracken (1989) identifies, brands have always drawn on the cultural world, including the so-called high culture of arts (most likely to be leveraged by luxury brands), as well as popular culture, and subcultures (such as various identity-based movements), They have also been part of culture, often co-opted or used by artists to make a particular point or by subcultures themselves who may see them as natural allies or enemies.

So what is the essence of Holt's claim and why does it matter? A parasite survives by feeding of its host, enjoying nourishment but rarely (if ever) giving anything back. For many cultures, this is how brands operate. Even those who promote brand authenticity, such as your authors, encourage brands to leverage links to culture as a way of enhancing associations. That said, we also make it clear that to do so requires one to act sincerely, lest one want to be called out as a brand poseur. One classic example is Pepsi's much maligned and short-lived 2017 brand campaign 'Live for now'. Featuring Kendall Jenner (as a sidenote, it's an interesting question what type of brand architecture the Jenner family operates by) giving up her seemingly superficial concerns to march with some protesters, the advertisement ends with the influencer handing a rather friendly looking riot policeman a can of Pepsi, presumably to release tensions. It's fair to ask why no protesters ever thought of this tactic before.

Why is this parasitism? The brand managers and their creative team co-opted the first wave of #blacklivesmatter protests for commercial ends. Since many of the protesters are overwhelmingly young and Pepsi's historic image has skewed younger and more 'on the moment' than its Atlanta-based rival Coke, trying to align with the values of its target was not in and of itself a bad thing. But and it is a big but, any hint of inauthenticity will get called out quickly on social media, and likely go viral globally. And these missteps can cost. Pepsi pulled the advertisement quickly after a backlash and suffered a sales decline subsequently as a result (Jenner apologized quickly and has continued to enjoy growth in her equity, suggesting the authenticity inherent in many person-brands gives one a substantive buffer in some cases).

Claims of parasitism arise in cases like these because the brand so obviously seeks to capitalize on a movement. McCracken's 1989 meaning transfer model is useful here. McCracken identified that brands connecting to culture benefit from the cultural associations, which helps enhance their meaning (essentially, they gain new associations), while the culture also gains some associations (which may be positive). However, big brands like Pepsi also need to play it safe, as they must appeal to supporters and detractors of such movements at the same time. So, the host culture gets diluted, with the core messaging of #blacklivesmatter removed in favor of protesters with placards calling for 'justice', or 'freedom', or being blurred out to obscure any message. The protesters themselves are young and beautiful, and certainly not particularly angry. They are well dressed, rather than prepared for encounters with riot police. The police themselves are calm, heroic, and again, amazingly fit and attractive. Is it any wonder charges of trivialization, white saviourism, and blatant commercialization resulted?

McCracken's model is correct as far as things go, brands are potential carriers of cultural meaning, and stand to gain from being so. And McCracken was a pioneer in bringing anthropology to the field of marketing and branding, a role he continues to embrace to this day. The mechanics of working with culture are now far more understood. McCracken (2010) calls for firms to develop Chief Culture Officers (CCOs), essentially corporate anthropologists (which could be seen as somewhat self-serving, if the logic wasn't so pervasive) that identify cultural movements and shifts. Critically, these CCOs then should 'go deep' on understanding the culture, identifying its ideals, norms, language, symbols, and so on. Why? Because as Holt says, brands need to transcend their natural parasitism and become cultural insiders.

Early studies often stressed how marketers could benefit from leveraging subcultures or even create brand communities that they control. Subsequent research quickly drew on the logic of legitimacy (which is seen by many as a resource to be gained and/or managed) to identify that brand managers had to earn the right to operate within the cultural space first. Steven Kates' (2004) pioneering work with LGBTQ community in North America identified the importance of brand's complying with normative litmus tests to be perceived as 'gay-friendly' and therefore authentic. Brands such as (the now struggling) Body Shop gained this status by using models living with HIV to normalize the disease, an issue of critical importance to the LGBTQ community at the time. Levi's had extended health insurance to its employees in same-sex relationships long before this became more common (the brand may have a very working man, blue-collar image, but during the 1970s became closely aligned with gay disco culture in the United States).

The actions of these brands meet Holt's call for citizen artistry, in so far as they contribute to the culture without expectation of return, and critically for those promoters of purpose or activist branding, do so quietly, without signaling their virtue. In contrast, brands that were judged not gay-friendly were those brands that were seen as insincere. The beer brand Coors was one of the most prominent villains in this regard, trying to gain listings in popular LGBTQ venues (which, *a la* McCracken, are critical cultural conduits for brands seeking to be perceived as 'cool' in the mainstream) while its owners simultaneously donated to the right-wing Heritage Foundation that was aggressively lobbying for anti-LGBTQ legislation. The brand was trying to literally have it both ways, and was quickly dropped from bars, with many LGBTQ venues proudly displaying 'No Coors served here' signs.

Coors was judged to be the ultimate cultural parasite, or poseur. Studies identify that inauthenticity is not just the absence of authenticity, but is in fact a moral judgment, viewed in terms of deception, dilution, and dishonesty (Silver et al. 2020). Holt, writing around the same time as *No Logo* was on the bestseller lists, was suggesting that brands could no longer act like Coors (Pepsi didn't seem to get the memo, but then again, many didn't), but instead needed to be more like Levi's and Body Shop in their relations to culture. While using culture as a resource is a feature of Holt's cultural branding model, he critically qualifies this by arguing brands must speak with cultural authority, which only comes from being an insider (hence the need for CCOs).

How does one do this? Much like an anthropologist entering the field in their focal community. One observes, one listens, one waits for something to happen, one tries to make sense of it all, and critically, one neither judges nor makes themselves the center of the story. One also avoids going native or perhaps more sensitively, becoming naturalized (literally a member of the subculture), a critical issue for brands wanting to authentically leverage culture for a mass audience. An early study on this process involved the consumer-led co-optation of faded Australian fashion icon, the Dunlop Volley shoe. Virtually dead as a brand, the shoes suddenly gained a newfound cool among Australian teenage dance culture.

Now any desperate brand manager would've been understandably tempted to develop a new line of rave shoes with supportive brand campaign and undoubtedly would've killed their legitimacy immediately, losing any chance of long-term revival. Instead, the team waited and watched. When asked for support, including advertising in local fanzines and providing shoes to be used by artists to make sculptures, they happily complied, with seemingly no commercial motives. They noted many dancers were graffitiing their shoes, often with profanities (which is why naturalizing is not a good idea – you cannot literally leverage these consumer-driven practices, nor you don't need to), which eventually led the team to develop a collaboration (long before the idea of 'collabs' became common) with a well-known graffiti artist. They made the shoes were available only in specialist stores in 'hip' neighborhoods and gave these stores an unprecedented level of product and advertising support. The dancers eventually moved on, but the brand's cool was established, and the less hip mainstream was ready to adopt a more consumer-friendly line (Beverland and Ewing 2005).

This is the insided-ness that Holt and others speak of when they call for brands to give up their cultural parasite status. Now there are still some challenges with this. Cultures may simply resist, and even go so far as to deliberately undermine marketer claims to subcultural authenticity (Arsel and Thompson 2011). Even the most culturally sensitive brands may have a damaging impact on cultural resources, especially if they are in short supply. For example, while surf brands have contributed much to surfing culture (many of their founders were long-standing members), the growth of surfing in Australia meant breaks became increasingly crowded, undermining the enjoyment many gained from the activity. And, whereas brands gain economically from their cultural insider status, the culture itself cannot capture the economic value of their own symbolic assets. This has led consumer ethicists to ponder how one can connect consumer culture and finance (Arvidsson and Peitersen 2013).

find your purpose! should brands be activists?

Nothing generates more polarized debate among practitioners than the call for brands to embrace a purpose. In many ways it's difficult to really pin down the meaning of brand purpose, and then meaningfully differentiate it from the brand's position or identity, or even the organization's wider mission. But apparently, at least to some, brands must have a purpose statement, and must definitely take a stand on key social issues. Unfortunately it would appear, customers, beyond a small vocal group, are rarely convinced. Shareholders seem even less impressed.

Brand purpose emerged after some questionable data demonstrated a relationship between brand success and engagement with social causes (Stengel 2011). The call went out for brand managers to take a stand on social issues, a strategy known as brand purpose or even brand activism. Some rewriting of history enables some to claim that purpose always lay at the heart of great brand management, with the oft-repeated example of the Lever Brothers (subsequently Unilever) developing Sunlight soap to improve hygiene among the world's masses. However, this founding goal suggests purpose is more about pursuing a higher order goal rather than more instrumental ends and has arguably motivated brand founders across many different categories. Writers such as David Aaker (2022) suggest that this is the true meaning of purpose, but this is far from the commonly held view of the term.

An interest in aligning brands with social causes has taken on greater urgency due to the way in which social media can mobilize a global audience around an important issue. The fallout of the Harvey Weinstein scandal that created the #metoo movement saw many brands rethink how they represented women in their advertising. Unilever, for example, worked with the UN's Representation of Women in Advertising group, reviewing all of their brand communications and finding some, particularly those by the locker-room lads' deodorant Axe, objectionable (arguably they had known this for years, but nonetheless the imagery of women falling at the feet of some male who sprayed more to get more had created a genuine power brand globally). At Gillette they arguably went further, flipping their famous 'The best a man can get' tagline to ask, 'Is this the best a man can be?' in an advert that blamed men for the sins of other men, before calling on them to do better. Not all men were convinced, with many switching to another shaving brand as a result (although the brand managed a necessary reposition with younger consumers). By themselves, these are not bad things, but arguably also represent exemplars of strategic revitalization to ensure these brands remain relevant to consumers as wider social values change.

Those embracing purpose seem to suffer from the same charges of inauthenticity or parasitism that Holt and others raise against brands leveraging culture. This shouldn't be that much of a surprise as the same process of co-optation is at work, with the addition of brands almost demanding to be praised for their newfound signals of virtue. Kates' examination of legitimacy is instructive here. Brands that were judged 'gay-friendly' in his study did not seek compensation or even praise for their actions, they simply undertook what we would now call 'activations' because they believed it was the right thing to do. In contrast, Ritson (2020b) provided his own simple and powerful litmus test for brands engaging in #blacklivesmatter activism when he presented the pictures of the management board of one such brand. Unsurprisingly they were all white and mostly male. With consumers, activists, and clever journalists auditing your claims, any purpose-based campaign needs to be subject to an internal audit logic before launch (this may not necessarily delay your launch, but it will change the tone of voice from virtue signaling to a more humble promise to improve).

Studies also reveal that authenticity involves perceptions of suffering or cost. That is, for brands, authenticity is not free. When Patagonia ran its famous Black Friday advertisement calling on consumers to not buy their jacket, but instead to make use of a range of more sustainable alternatives, they were sacrificing profits for principle (don't worry, the advert actually resulted in a sales jump in said jacket). Likewise, when Levi's ended its lucrative relationship with the Boy Scouts of America because the latter had banned gay scoutmasters, it came with real financial cost and backlash from more conservative stakeholders including consumers (Kates 2004).

Toughing it out matters, as Gillette found when it doubled down on shifting images of masculinity over several iterations of its campaign. While it was urged by many to pull back, it decided to let its aging angry customers go, in favor of attracting younger men who were the future of the brand. Why it remains an example of how not to do purpose is beyond us. The brand started by recognizing it hardly had the right to lecture anyone on toxic masculinity given its history of advertising around the 'Best a man can get' tagline, so worked with domestic violence charities and other like-minded organizations as part of a program of change, while acknowledging its own complicity. Purpose and activism are subject to the same standards as cultural branding and need to be approached sensitively and with a long-term view.

global vs. local

There was a time when global mass-market brands came to define the future of the globe. George Ritzer (1983) used the term 'McDonaldization' as a metaphor to capture the idea that trade liberalization would decrease the importance of local differences, paving the way for brands to become more efficient, offering one single vision, in one single language to the entire world. Economically, such a move has some attraction. Lower marketing costs, a larger, loyal audience open to the possibilities of endless extensions, and even a decrease in local product variants all make sense. On the other hand, it is perhaps no surprise that the term McDonaldization and indeed the brand's (that never auditioned for the role of global corporate octopus) 'Mc' prefix became bywords among the burgeoning anti-globalization movement for all that was wrong with the world. While global branding was once *the* future, research reveals the present picture is far more complicated, especially given the rise of nationalism in the past decade.

More recently, McDonaldization has given way to another brand metaphor, eBayization (Ahuvia and Izberk-Bilgin 2011), to reflect the more bottom-up, fragmented nature of global branding in which social media platforms provide the basis for consumers to connect to one another from around the globe. Why the shift? Well, much of the historic debate around globalization and branding has reflected a pro-Western, center–periphery logic whereby it is taken-for-granted that large Western brands will be doing the globalizing, at the expense of presumably less valued, less professionally managed local brands in the Global South (who are believed to suffer the disadvantage of their country-of-origin image). This idea was captured in the 1999 bestseller by Thomas Friedman *The Lexus and the Olive Tree*, in which the power of the brand would sweep away the locally rooted olive tree. The novel idea of the book was called the Golden Arches Theory of Peace, based on the observation that no two countries with McDonalds outlets have gone to war (which has been falsified many times). This was written at the tail end of triumphant claims about the end of history and dominance of neo-liberal economics and democracy, which presently, given the re-emergence of nationalism and decline of support for democracy, look rather quaint. Turns out that olive trees have very deep tap roots, and that local culture, while potentially tolerant of global interlopers, is unlikely to be swept away by them (olive trees are also rather long-lived, something Friedman forgot).

Our good colleague Donald Lancaster (presently an academic at University of Exeter and in a past life, an experienced brand strategist) characterizes the global vs. local debate in terms of a trade-off between efficiency and effectiveness. As one of the team behind HSBC's iconic World's Local Bank campaign (which helped make the bank a global financial player), he argued that being completely global is very efficient but may come at the cost of local meaning, whereas completely local is high on meaning but low on efficiency. For marketers seeking to build a global brand, finding some type of happy medium is essential, especially given the realities of budgetary constraints and the opportunity to have a global brand franchise. Describing the development of HSBC's campaign, it becomes clear that seeking this happy medium enhances creativity rather than constraining it. In the case of HSBC, the desire for global efficiency resulted in comparing the bank's logo to universally accepted symbols such as power sockets, stop signs, hospitality, and so on, and enabled the bank to play up its global scope and local depth.

eBayization rejects the center–periphery approach to globalization in favor of what has been labelled deterritorialization (Sharifonnasabi et al. 2020). Deterritorialization removes the very idea of a center or a periphery, instead arguing for a multiplicity of connections, in which culture can often be disconnected from the notion of place. This may sound complicated, but you probably experience this every day. For example, recently there has been the emergence of restaurants advertising themselves as Berliner Döner. For those who don't know, döner is a Turkish meat-based dish, consisting of meat and salad, which can be served in several ways. So why the disconnecting of this dish from its Turkish roots? Well, the Berliner Döner reflects the large Turkish immigrant population in Berlin, who have put their own spin on the traditional dish originally to appeal to non-Turkish Berliners. Here traditions have been transplanted, or deterritorialized from their source, to produce new forms of culture.

In branding terms this also happens. Australians and New Zealanders have not only developed chains of branded coffee shops, serving classics such as flat whites and brunch, but also bringing a tradition of specialty coffee to new markets. Many of these are no longer run by antipodean immigrants but simply adopt the cultural ethos to appeal to local consumers who see these brands as both local and global. Brands of cosmetics regularly launch collections to reflect holiday traditions around the world such as Chinese New Year collections that are launched globally and which often then become part of the non-lunar calendar elsewhere. Influences such as Korean pop, Nigerian and Turkish drama, and Scandinavian noir all demonstrate how platform brands such as Netflix have helped export cultural connections globally. These genres, plus their adoption by other nations' film studios reflect the logic of eBayization rather than McDonaldization (where Hollywood primarily exported content to the world).

Brand researchers have spent considerable time examining the tensions surrounding globalization and brands, uncovering a plethora of ways in which consumers embrace, twist, or reject global brands for identity purposes. In parts of the Middle East, for example, global brands are often framed by nationalist movements as 'infidels' to be rejected in favor of local variants. Paradoxically, these local brand variants often copy many of the assets of the global brand (Mecca Cola, for example), while subverting them with twists that enable locals to reinforce their collective identity through their use (Izberk-Bilgin 2012). Lest you think a backlash against globalization is underway, other researchers have identified how local consumers may embrace global brands for nationalist reasons. Chinese consumers, for example, were found to embrace high-end Western brands because their ability to purchase these luxury items reflected the triumph of their country's economic model (i.e., Western brands were viewed as being desperate to appeal to consumers in a new global order, arguably with China back at the center). But not all Chinese consumers were so minded, with some rejecting global brands in favor of locally made products precisely because global brands had moved manufacturing to China, which again, reflected a newfound assertiveness among local consumers about their economic might (Dong and Tian 2009).

Deterritorialization also encourages us to think about the meanings of global and local from the viewpoint of the consumer, rather than historic geopolitical positions. And while you may think that is a good thing, your experience as a brand manager is about to get a whole lot of more complicated. For example, one alternate to globalization has been glocalization, whereby global brands typically make some allowance for local culture, either through product variants or in terms of communications. Despite its name, glocalization is still rooted in center–periphery distinctions (it is only global Western brands doing the local adaptation) but is perhaps less naïve than advocates for a globalized, one-size-fits-all brand. However, local adaptation can create a backlash elsewhere, reflecting both the potential for polysemy (i.e., a multiplicity of meanings), and speed with which information can flow via social media (usually stripped of local context and subtlety).

One such example involved global stalwart KFC that practices glocalization not only with product adaptation but also in terms of its sponsorship activities. In Australia, KFC has long sponsored touring West Indies cricket teams. The rivalry between the West Indies and Australia goes back to the 1970s and 1980s when the two sides represented the dominant powers in cricket. A sport played in summer, the so-called Summer of Cricket was a shared cultural ritual for most Australians who revere their sporting heroes and also embrace rivalry with equally passionate teams and groups of fans. So what went wrong? KFC had long run advertisements featuring West Indian cricketers and also their touring fans, all of whom were featured enjoying fried chicken while watching or after playing cricket. However, one advertisement featuring a lone, white Australian fan sitting in the West Indies stand created a backlash, not in Australia, but in the United States, where cultural meanings around fried chicken can take on a different meaning. The advert featured said fan looking grim, thinking that he was going to be in for a long day as West Indies greats tore through the Aussie batting order, or destroyed the bowling attack with their swashbuckling batting. The solution, share a bucket of KFC and everyone could get on and enjoy the party.

For Australians, the message was clear – despite the on-field rivalry, everyone could come together as 'mates' and enjoy fried chicken during the summer. African Americans, for whom this cultural context did not apply, interpreted the advert to have a much more sinister meaning – a lone white man looking frightened, placates Black people with fried chicken (a trope that long had racist connotations in the United States). No amount of pointing out the cultural differences in meaning would convince consumers in the United States and, facing the reality of the vast differences in size and economic power between Australian and African American consumers,

KFC Australia pulled the long-running campaign (Puntoni et al. 2010). Turns out the center has some bite after all.

Similarly, while deterritorialization sounds like a more enlightened approach to global relations and branding, some may not be so happy when local icons start to adapt to new waves of immigrant consumers. The olive tree does have strong roots, and recently academics have been identifying that reterritorialization can make life even more complicated for well-meaning brand managers. Luedicke's (2015) study of what he called Austrian indigenes, or white Austrians who could trace their roots back many centuries to the nation, identified how brands seeking to adapt to new migrant groups, even naturalized locals, could fall foul of a nationalist backlash. Whereas local retailers spot an opportunity to appeal to immigrant tastes and arguably those indigenes more comfortable with immigration and globalization, a nationalist backlash can emerge among other indigenes who see this as a dilution of their culture and the betrayal of brands they and their forebears have long supported.

Others have noted that the rise of biculturalism has opened up possibilities for brand managers willing to embrace complexity and paradox. Paradox brands by definition straddle conflicting or oppositional meanings, and may appeal to bicultural consumers, such as Asian Americans or Black Britons, because such groups of consumers have always negotiated two, often contradictory, cultural worlds. This cognitive flexibility, which may come from working between two languages and/or two sets of cultural values and rituals, leads bicultural consumers be more attracted to brands that might embrace multiple personalities, such as rugged and sophisticated (Land Rover) or traditional but trendy (Burberry) rather than more single-dimensional brands (Rodas et al. 2021). Although the authors suggest that this may upend traditional approaches to positioning (which is seen as very singular), often such paradoxes are at the heart of brand authenticity, in which brands must be both timeless and relevant, or anti-commercial yet appealing, and so on.

On the authenticity question, globalization, particularly in relation to the offshoring of manufacturing, has resulted in an expansion of counterfeiting and its impact on the image and revenue of the affected brands. With many brands often offshoring production to countries with legal systems that offer less protection for intellectual property (at least for non-locals), it has been noted that the same factory producing the branded original is also producing the counterfeit item, often to the same, or even better quality specifications. This has triggered a whole consumer culture of experts dedicated to identifying the original. At the same time, purchases of counterfeits are often a middle-class phenomenon, with consumers buying them for fun, alongside the original (for fear of theft or damage), or for anti-capitalist motives. Culturally, what is counterfeit and authentic is also highly contextualized. A study in Vietnam, for example, finds that consumers distinguish between branded goods, copy goods, and fake goods. While the branded is the original, copy goods are simply functional counterfeits that provide the same services at a lower price. These goods often help younger consumers embrace brands without earning their parents' ire for being profligate with their funds. Fake goods are simply those counterfeits that provide no actual function such as perfume that is just water or counterfeit phones that simply do not work at all (Vann 2006).

The angst that emerged with the explosion of counterfeiting resulted in much talk about the need for greater legal protection for larger brands. However, no local politician is going to threaten local businesses who are providing employment and potentially other, personal benefits, in favor of some global interloper. Some nations also actively use counterfeiting as a strategy of technology transfer (although in truth this has been going on since time immemorial). Now, a more nuanced view has emerged. Within some categories such as luxury fashion, it's now an open secret that many of the larger brands unofficially sanction some counterfeiters and focus solely on trying to control those who work outside of this legal grey area. It's also been pointed out that counterfeiting, although perhaps not a sincere form of flattery, nonetheless says something about the power of your brand. That is, not being counterfeited is worse than being counterfeited. Counterfeits in this view may simply be a pathway to eventual ownership of the real item and should be actively tolerated. Others go so far as to co-opt counterfeiters, often developing collaborations with them as part of a long tradition of conquering counterculture by embracing it.

So what does all this complexity mean for brand managers? Well, first, whether you like it or not, social media means you are likely to be on a global stage at some point in the life of your brand. Second, while this has the potential for backlash via polysemy, it also represents an opportunity both for cultural appreciation while also benefiting from the efficiency that comes with globalization. With more and more consumers exposed to brand messaging and consumer culture around the globe, the one-size-fits-all brand may be about to make a surprising comeback in many markets. Third, understanding cultural differences, at the local and global level, requires greater connection with your customers and the lived reality of their lives. Since identity goals can give rise to both individual and collective jobs to be done, isolating consumers from the wider context in which they operate will lead to unexpected backlash but also lost opportunities.

a branded world?

Where the preserve of brands was once mainly related to products (notwithstanding the unsupported claim that the Catholic Church is the oldest brand in history), branding has spread to almost all aspects of life. Today countries, cities, regions, and even neighborhoods are brands. Personal branding has expanded well beyond celebrity to include everyday humble influencers whose supposed authentic lifestyle is actually a product of tightly controlled brand metrics. Government departments, charities, sports teams, cultural organizations, and even anti-branding or anti-capitalist movements have all succumbed to the logic of brand personality, archetypes, and of course assets. But is this a good thing? And if so, good for whom?

Certainly there's been benefits. Branding can help enhance the reputation of charities and therefore drive more donations. Influencer work has opened up opportunities for many young people to live a lifestyle they could have never dreamed of. Cities and regions can benefit from greater tourism and investment. But clearly all is not well. Residents of many tourist hotspots such as Venice, Barcelona, Amsterdam, and Copenhagen are rebelling against overtourism, electing mayors and parties with an explicitly pro-resident stance. Central to many of these residents' complaints is the impact of the ubiquitous short-term rental platform brand AirbnB, which stands accused of raising rents, depleting the stock of available houses for the very people who often make the place unique and interesting for tourists in the first place, and generally making residents' lives hell. British visitors to Amsterdam looking to enjoy the city's brand attributes (usually featured in specialty 'coffee' shops) are tracked online and given information that such activities are illegal, while some city residents have put up official-looking but fake warning signs saying certain areas are 'no-go' for tourists because of the risk of theft or assault (or worse, being forced to eat local delicacies such as tompouce and bitterballen).

Concern with protection of the brand has also become a common theme in many large-scale scandals within government departments, playing a role in ignoring and disciplining whistleblowers in the Countess of Chester Hospital neonatal unit scandal, where a nurse was found guilty of the murder of eight babies and attempted murder of a further 10 (at the time of writing). One of the United Kingdom's most trusted brands, the Royal Mail, has been brought low by their treatment of sub-postmasters in the Horizon scandal. Again, the desire to protect brand image rather than investigate potentially brand-trashing allegations has often driven managers to look the other way when they shouldn't.

The dream of person branding also isn't always sweetness and light. The personality cults that build around politicians, CEOs, and disgraced tech and cultural sector executives (among many others) blind people to their weaknesses and even crimes. Studies also show that the authenticity so coveted by brand partners forces influencers to provide ever more emotionally extreme content, often resulting in serious impacts on their mental health and personal lives. The need for more and more intimate content via opening the truly real backstage of life as Goffman discusses provides little private space for person-brands, leading to breakdowns, feelings of alienation, and self-harm (Heeris Christensen et al. 2024).

Have we gone too far with brands? Cities and countries are rich, messy expressions of centuries of culture, they shift and change over time, often in unexpected ways. Brands on the other hand operate according to a rigid consistency logic, emphasizing the need to eliminate the off-brand elements while reinforcing core attributes. Think about this for a second. This sounds less like a democracy and more like an authoritarian regime. Do we want our living spaces free from so-called undesirable elements, or have the rich aspects of our lives removed to please tourists (and do even visitors want this?)? Similarly, we rail against artists who never change, never challenge themselves and play safe, yet why do we take up Tom Peters' suggestion to build 'the brand that is you'? Are we more or less interesting when we live our public lives performing to a very tight script? Remember Byron Sharp's warning here, customers get bored with brands fairly quickly, so is staying on-brand as a person good for anything other than online dating sites?

what about the dark arts?

Branding is a powerful tool. Technically it's also a neutral one, in so far as it will work for those seeking to do good or just provide something useful, to those seeking domination and control, through to those operating in shall we say, morally greyer areas of the economy.

Fans of serial brand *Breaking Bad* will know that Walter White was not immune to using branding to enhance his legend and status, including the distinct blue of his ultra-pure crystal meth, his 'Heisenberg' moniker, and his pork pie hat. So successful was his strategy, that his personal brand outlived the serial brand, being licensed for a range of t-shirts, coffee mugs, and at time of writing, a Walter's Coffee Roastery in Istanbul. Criminals have always used branding, often as a means of power, at least if Hollywood et al. are to be believed.

There are vast swathes of economic activity that also use brands that may be, shall we say, morally questionable. We are not just talking about the usual suspects of tobacco, booze, fast food, guns, and K-pop, but also about those innocuous services of private security or even mercenary armies with nondescript names, such as the Wagner Group, G4S, Blackwater (which went through a range of name changes), all of which have logos and an array of supporting brand assets that presumably mean something to their government clients across the globe. Many of these brands seem so bland, one is tempted to ignore them altogether. What could they possibly stand for? What is their main promise, or function? That is of course the point. Gone are the days when state-tolerated mercenaries have idiosyncratic names such as Keenie Meenie Services. Whereas many criminals go legit through money laundering acquisitions, bland names of less savory organizations enable one to hide in plain sight, or at least behind a typically nondescript name that could only be dreamed up by boring corporate types.

If you are reading this, you probably have some interest in brands. We're reminded of an MBA class we taught where the favorite brands of each of the executives were the ones that made them the most money. There was no room for sentiment in that context. But even younger, less experienced students have asked us 'what does all this consuming for identity really mean?' Jokingly, one of us replied 'it's meaningless in a sense, but knowing it can help you make money', which brought a knowing smile and much greater focus on the materials from students. Now business school academics have always shilled for 'the man' but branding can have downsides. We cover some of these below, but apart from the application of branding to industries with, shall we say, somewhat problematic associations, creating demand for the 'it brand' or 'it product' has created some very real social problems.

While a new wave of street luxury brands may delight in seeing queues outside their stores hours before an official 'drop', reports of youngsters being robbed or even murdered for their much-coveted shoes are not uncommon, resulting in newspaper headlines and even documentaries such as Yemi Bamiro's 2020 *One Man and His Shoes* (whether this is a case of all publicity is good publicity is another thing, certainly the practices of hyping up drops has not stopped). By hyping up demand for branded items and making their ownership so integral to the identity of younger people (who let's face it, are impressionable), brand managers may have some complicity in the consequences. In many cases, the hype begets the reality of items that post-drop are often readily available.

Similarly, reports of young women in South-East Asia trading sexual favors for luxury goods (provided for by older men) are as concerning as they are unsurprising (particularly in cultural contexts where luxury is more about fitting in with a narrative of personal success than standing out as an individual). In China, the ownership of the right luxury bag is essential for young women (in particular) to demonstrate their success and gain access to employment. Fournier would label such relationships as an abusive partner, while culturally, such bags become stereotyped as 'secretary's bags', which although good for short-term sales, ultimately harms the brand's image and requires a rethink around the size and placement of brand assets such as logos.

Brands can certainly create addiction-like behaviors. By this we don't mean the medical models of addiction that underpin consumption of cigarette or alcohol brands (although for alcoholics often the overwhelming need for a hit renders the brand irrelevant), and if serial brands such as Breaking Bad and The Wire are to be believed, narcotics. Earlier in the text we explained how self-authentication underpins brand choice and authenticity underpins motives behind consumption. The potential dark side for these behaviors is obvious – if it's about being your true self or your desired self, then how far will you go to fulfil this need? At least one study identifies that outcomes may include financial difficulties, eating disorders, theft, and self-hate (Chung et al. 2018).

In 2024, some put-out (and very rich) shoppers in the United States threatened to sue luxury brand Hermés because of their well-known practice of rationing the perennial it-bag Birkin to customers who had already spent several thousand dollars on less desirable items (Guardian March 20, 2024). In this case we may have less sympathy and certainly the courts are likely to take a dim view on such a case (at least one would hope), but in an age where who we are is a function of what we own (and increasingly, are able to access), some scenario planning around negative consequences of hype might be worthwhile.

While such outcomes are the result of marketer-driven hype, some brands have also been adopted as uniform by, shall we say, nontarget users. Toyota regularly has to deny connections to listed terrorist groups, largely because their pick-up trucks are extremely durable, easy to fix, and lend themselves to be fitted out with rockets and anti-aircraft guns. Every news report that features images from the field with these groups also builds an association, at least in the mind of some US politicians, that the brand isn't doing enough to restrict sales to the wrong target users.

Long-time advocate for racial harmony, former World No. 1 tennis player Fred Perry was presumably turning in his grave when one of his shirts was adopted as a uniform by a high-profile far-right group in the United States. This process was given the label 'hate-jacking'. While many consumers took to social media to vent how they'd never use the brand again, others fired back that the brand's founder had a long history of fighting racial prejudice. While the marketing team discontinued the shirt design in the United States, it used the episode to remind the world of its heritage.

Whereas one feels for brands such as Fred Perry (who, like many sportspeople, stretched the founder's personal brand into the product realm), other brands suffering the same adoptions are probably asking for it. Start-up skiwear brand Pit Viper's overt misogyny probably made it a likely target for hate-jacking by the far right and undermined the brand team's response of 'not supporting hate'. Nonetheless, handled well, such nontarget adoptions can provide a crisis-induced turning point for the brand team. Pit Viper eventually decided that aligning the brand more openly with LGBTQ and Drag events was one way to make the brand a turn-off for the hate groups.

Within the purpose and activism literatures or even practice discourses, there is also an obvious left wing or liberal bias in the treatment of the social causes that brands align with. While consumer research is all too often littered with topics that appeal to an overwhelmingly middle-class group of scholars, it is surprising that practitioners seek so readily to align with causes that are typically more liberal politically, especially during the 2020s where polarization has been on the increase. There are brands, such as fast-food provider Chick-fil-A, that wear their Christian morals on their brand asset sleeves, refusing to open on Sunday and being open about their lack of support for LGBTQ causes (in favor of 'traditional families'). Since these are the founders' principles and they operate within red ocean markets, it's fair to say they would make an interesting cause célèbre.

With activism leading to more polarization, it's also fair to say that marketers can potentially start harming the causes they seek to align with. In 2023, Budweiser Lite got caught up in a political storm around their use of trans model Dylan Mulvaney as one of their many influencers. While the brand had long used a diverse array of influencers without any pushback, heightened political polarization in the United States has resulted in greater sensitivity among audiences on issues that can be framed in left/right terms. The brand not only lost sales and its market dominance (and continued to do so a year on) but also diminished support among marketers in general for Pride events (Liaukonyte et al. 2023). Likewise aging-Punk beer brand BrewDog may have sought to cynically exploit workers' rights and health and safety concerns in Qatar during the 2022 FIFA World Cup, but two years on the plight of these workers remains unchanged, while countries with similar records have been accused of sportswashing by buying up professional sports team brands.

Purpose-based branding can result in other unintended, but perhaps not unforeseeable consequences. The common approach of making consumers, or even budget-stretched public services such as law enforcement, responsible for these consequences can ring hollow in an age of aspirational brand imagery and claims of higher brand purpose. This process, called responsibilization, has been identified as a favored way for corporations to shift responsibility for the downsides (or what economists might call externalities) of capitalism onto consumers themselves (Giesler and Veresiu 2014). Policy-wise this has the effect of shifting the conversation away from the need to impose more taxes or regulations on corporates and at an extreme, as observed by late comedian Bill Hicks quoted earlier, creates new markets for targeting (such as green, bottom-of-the-pyramid, and conscious consumers).

are brands really (always) about identity? (or, 'I'm not really a brand person')

Have you ever met that 'I'm not really a brand person?' As an icebreaker for our classes we often ask students (of all ages and experience levels), 'name a brand you most admire and tell us why'. Even for a class on brand management, you'd be surprised how many times we get told 'I'm not really a brand person, but...' (usually followed by a list of well-known mass-market brand for a variety of often quite emotional reasons). In some classes we continue the exercise, splitting people up into pairs and asking each partner to identify all the brands the other has with them. The exercise is futile in some respects because the non-brand-person simply counters that they were bought for rational reasons or because they cannot be avoided. The second point we are willing to concede, but we'd challenge anyone wearing a sports team's merchandise on the rationality of their choice.

How true is the claim that people, at least in contexts where they have the necessities to live, are not buying for identity reasons? This is a difficult question to answer because most of the results for or against the identity claim are often a function of how the question is asked or how the research is done. If you, as we did, ask the question of what brand do you like and why, you will generate pretty dull, surface-level answers. For example, the most common answer to our question is the brand Apple. Asked why they like it students mostly point to ease of use and the design. Could they do otherwise? Given that we asked them to process a preference consciously, probably not. That is, the reasons that they like the design may have something to do with the brand's claim to 'think different' and that may appeal because of some desired identity (despite the fact that it seems many Apple fans think different by following a large herd of like-minded others, so much so that brand ownership has become associated with a certain persona in satirical publications).

This type of approach is typical of large-scale surveys that report how consumers see little difference between the brands they buy and conclude that searching for points of difference is relatively futile. Influential advocates, usually drawing on the work of the Ehrenberg–Bass group, note that consumers buy brands for fairly mundane, usually pragmatic reasons. One might be tempted to retort that they study fast-moving consumer goods (FMCG) goods so how much identity do we expect behind the purchase of one brand of baked beans over the next? There are exceptions to this. One, culturally minded researchers have found an enormous array of meaning underpinning the decision to buy FMCGs (including notions of collective identity), and Ehrenberg–Bass have found consistent results across seemingly much richer brands, such as services or luxury goods. Ask a simple question, with a simple method, and you often just barely scratch the surface.

But the opposite is also true for those, like Fournier (and indeed us), who explore brand meaning through a mix of projective techniques and life interviews. The same goes for those using ethnographic methods to unpack the deeper communal bonds around branding. If you ask someone to develop a collage of what the brand means to them, then you will get deeper answers than if you just asked directly. For example, in our work on authenticity, using photo-elicitation techniques, we identified that some brands offer authenticity through providing a sense of control. This underpinned a preference for brands strong on provable functional performance. For these consumers, the brand was authentic if it worked as promised. You may of course think, 'aha!' not an identity motive. But, in their accompanying depth interviews these consumers recounted many stories of how they were in control in often very tricky situations. As Holt might say, their brand choices enabled them to enact the action hero identity they desired.

One often-repeated objection also concerns those pillars of rationality and instrumentality, business-to-business buyers. All the textbooks on B2B note that business buyers are simply more rational, price-focused, and must follow the rules set down by their organizations. The idea of buying for safety, status, friendship, and any other identity-related value rarely enters the world of academic B2B marketing research. But one does wonder why these highly rational organizations have to put in complex rules to ensure purchasing managers do the right thing. In the late 1990s, the first author while visiting a wine industry tradeshow noticed that a brand of grape harvesters was being displayed by semi-naked women, a practice that used to be common, suggesting that organizations were right to put some rules around their buyers. Could it be that at best, business buyers must be forced to be rational against their will?

Well, the Industrial Marketing & Purchasing Group (IMP) pioneered an understanding of business buyer behavior that was anything but rational. Purchasing managers were often part of complex webs of relationships, stretching back years, that were framed around reciprocity. As the very old saying goes, 'No one ever got fired by buying IBM'. This is not so much a statement about the strengths of that brand as it is about a purchasing manager using the brand to cover their arse if anything goes wrong. And, since IBM was once the epitome of the corporate man (so much so that Apple was founded on the promise that buyers would 'never be part of the machine', IBM being said machine), could it be that one becomes part of that august club when one buys the brand?

Similarly, studies have identified the value of all those inter-company golf days and outings, largely as a way of strengthening bonds between sellers and buyers, or now, brands and customers. Business buyers may not view B2B brands as friends in Fournier terms, but they certainly are not immune to other influences, some of which most certainly reflect a desire for professional status (i.e., identity).

So where does this leave us? Postmodernity certainly has at least partially disconnected identity from more stable notions, but this only created anxiety about one's place in the world and one's status relative to others. Brands filled this role. Spurred on by the success of *No Logo* and various anti-globalization protests, the anti-brand identity took root, and was even reinforced by *No Logo*'s own brand of nonbrand Converse look-alike trainers. Likewise, 'I'm not a brand person' might simply be an identity claim, that one is not persuaded by emotional brand appeals, but is much closer to rational economic consumer lionized by textbooks. But this too, can be positioned as just another identity. Maybe all this concern with identity is overdone, with even Holt arguing that consumers bond to brands in rather simple, albeit identity-driven, ways. And we should always keep in the mind the call for distinctiveness of benefits as well as the centrality of points of parity (which are invariably functional) to brand strength.

do brands make us crazy, or stupid?

You're just buying that for the brand! Remember being told that by your parents? We both do. And yes, one of us can admit that the small red dot that signifies the Leica brand is certainly a reason to shell out a lot of money for a camera that has several just as good, if not better, cheaper counterparts. The other author is very much an admirer of Tom Ford sunglasses, with their distinctive and subtle 'T' built into the frame and arm. Again, there are probably better sunglasses in terms of function, but that's to miss the point. The answer to the accusation is 'of course we are, we all do'.

Do brands affect the way we think though? The answer is yes. One simple example should suffice. Since Apple remains one of the world's most valuable brands (at least at the time of writing – we may regret this claim if the book remains in print for many years), in class we like have students explore the ways in which the brand communicates effectively. At some point, after hearing about technology, founders, myths, iconic advertisements (the 1984 Macintosh one is good, 2024's Crush!, less so), connections to the creative sector, the retail stores and platforms, we interrupt and ask, 'what is the most effective communication tool this tech giant has ever developed?' Students usually scratch their heads and give up. We argue it is the humble analog sticker that comes with every Apple product (although as the brand has grown in value, they've become stingier with add-ons, so now that even basic peripherals are extra, maybe they're charging for stickers too). This sticker is used by Apple fans to signal their allegiance with the brand and because the stickers have changed as the brand's logo has changed, possessing a collection of them signals the length of a consumer's loyalty. It's not unheard of for Apple fans to carefully scrape off their stickers from the back windscreen when they are trading in their vehicles in for an upgrade. But the sticker has even more power than this.

Reports that consumers would put a sticker on their non-Apple phone began to circulate in the late 2000's, following the release of the brand's breakthrough smartphone. Consumers would not only add the sticker to their Nokia or Motorola (or other similarly less-smart phone), but also report that their rebranded phone now worked better, and get this, felt cooler. While we associate brands with marketing, we often forget that marketing is customer-centric, with a more reactive stance (i.e., it wants to give the customer what they want), while branding is a tool that actively tries to shape how we think, feel, and behave. Brands are tools we use to get consumers to do what we want, so we can sell them stuff they may not have known they need, for prices that would have felt ridiculous if the brand was absent.

Consumer psychologists have demonstrated the power of brands to impact our cognitive processes. Once exposed to the brands, we begin to change our preferences, literally going into 'brand mode' when faced with a consumption decision. For example, if we subliminally expose consumers to known thrift brands, such as Aldi or Primark, then consumers become more focused on seeking out low-priced options

(Rahinel et al. 2021). The brand actually shapes the subsequent decision-making process. And yes, exposure to the Apple logo results in a preference for creativity, whereas the IBM logo has the opposite effect. Red Bull may not literally give you wings, but exposure to the logo will make you more aggressive. These occur because the brand comes with a network of associations that we know because of repeated exposure over time. The brand literally is influencing us to think in ways that marketers would desire.

This may all sound quite terrifying, especially to those of you who remember James Vicary's claim that messages saying 'drink Coke' embedded within films led to greater sales of said soda (Packard 1957). Although his claims were eventually labelled unreliable, which is a nice way of saying no one else could reproduce the results (largely because the messages were a little too subliminal for anyone to actually pick up on, consciously or subconsciously), it's certainly the case that prolonged exposure to hyperreal environments where brands are everywhere does seem to be having an effect, although this effect is a lot more nuanced and complex than just getting people to buy more sugary (or now, sugar-free) soft drinks.

But are consumers simple dupes when it comes to brands? This lies at the heart of the claim we started this section with and is often why people buying things for labels alone are derided. One response to the consumer-as-dupe claim is to push back and point out that just because consumers understand what well-known brands stand for, it doesn't mean they are stupid or lacking agency. If they were, the marketers of these brands would have a much easier time of things, not suffering repeat failures in new product or service launches or running advertising campaigns that do not land as intended.

Likewise, consumers are capable of reframing brands in numerous ways, which suggests they have a clear understanding of important a brand's image is, and therefore how damaging it can be if they call it out. Parodies are common within the brand sphere, so much so that some brands even do it themselves. Papers examining Starbucks and the new coffee culture have noted how consumers opposed to the brand encroaching on neighborhood coffee shops would repurpose the famed mermaid logo with the term 'corporate whore' underneath it. A quick search on brand parodies on the internet (we used Google by the way) will reveal lots of cool content that flips the brand's desired image: McDonalds becomes McDiabetes, Dell becomes Hell, Amazon becomes Moneyzgone (with the clever addition of the smiling arrow being turned upside down into a frown), while Coca-Cola is rewritten as Cocaine, which does at least have some indexical connection to the brand's past.

These parodies even have a name in brand research: the doppelgänger image. A doppelgänger is like your evil identical twin, and in branding, studies have shown that consumers will take a brand's core characteristic and reframe it, stripping it of all its marketing niceties (is anyone really 'lovin'' McDonalds?) to highlight the brand's truer evil intentions. Markus Giesler (2012) argues that these parodies or culture jams can and must be managed carefully by brand managers. By this, he does not mean trying to shut them down, but to recognize that they may impact on the consumer–brand relationship. Therefore the brand must adapt, providing an answer to the parody in a way that allows the consumer to keep their relationship going.

Sounds good, and the perpetually youthful-looking Markus demonstrated this with a longitudinal, and we must say brilliant (Markus is extremely connected in the world of academic marketing) examination of the Botox brand. Markus noticed that Botox had essentially become normalized in his Toronto neighborhood, and he began to examine how this occurred (normalizing or mainstreaming a previously fringe consumer practice is a great marketing strategy, as it often creates a blue ocean category in which you have the lead). What he actually found was more interesting. The Botox brand was constantly contested, with those who used it effectively caught in the middle. The job of the brand team was to constantly pivot to counter these contests, providing users with new identity-driven messaging to enable them to feel good about the brand.

For example, whereas consumers initially saw Botox as a form of fun, something they did together at a Botox party, media reports began to suggest it was poisonous (technically it is of course but the dose is very low and even water will kill you in the wrong amount), which obviously started to prey on the minds of users. So the brand was reframed in terms of being a miracle of medicine that allowed you to age gracefully. Consumers were delighted and sales grew. But actress Nicole Kidman was accused of having a frozen face in one of her many movies, which became a meme, again not something users wanted to hear or discuss. So they pivoted again, reframing the brand as the expression of your authentic self without the judgment suffered by women as they age. This continued over the years and despite the constant parodying, the brand team creatively reworked the narrative, strengthening the connection with loyalists and attracting new users along the way. Botox made billions, although rumor has it, they were too cheap to pay the US$35 to access Giesler's 2012 *Journal of Marketing* article, with the CEO's secretary tasked with ringing him urgently in the early hours of the morning to get a free copy. We're guessing they had a quarterly earnings target to meet, and every dollar counted.

Another answer to the 'are consumers dupes?' question is that consumers play along. We will cover this is our discussion of authenticity earlier in the guide, but also note Holt's (2004) view that the reason sciency branding seems to work is consumers are very well versed in identifying what brands stand for and if they are so bothered, will fill out tracking surveys and nod along in focus groups accordingly. Whether they truly buy in or even connect with the brand in any meaningful way, let alone do so in the way intended by brand marketers, is another thing altogether. Holt's cultural brand model relies on the rejection of a more abstract intellectual connection to the brand, in favor of more powerful, identity-based reasons.

Of course, it could be that we really have been duped, or taken over by aliens seeking to keep us under control.

chapter summary

We've provided what we see as some of the enduring challenges around branding. There are undoubtedly more (issues of representation are just one area that deserves more attention and care), and also more to come (what impact will advances in artificial intelligence have on creativity or even points of difference/distinctiveness, for example?). We'd also like to think that some challenges might slowly dissipate as brand managers embrace a more pluralistic view of so-called best practice, both in terms of strategy and tactics. Co-creation also means that challenges around identity are likely to flare up more often, especially as brand managers attempt to appeal to identity-based segments, leverage consumer and ethnic culture, while also meeting financial targets and trying to appeal to other, perhaps even oppositional groups as part of a mass-market strategy. Fortunately, challenges beset by paradox are the gold standard of academic contribution thresholds and often the path to financial reward. We hope however that the solution largely lies in more pluralistic views of theories, methods, and practices.

6
Epilogue

Well, you reached the end. Hopefully the journey was worth it. We hope we got our target market right and positioned the book correctly. We also hope the execution wasn't too off, or at least hit the mark most of the time (the title does require us to only be *fairly* interesting). In our view, brands matter, not just because we are marketers or consumers but because they're interesting in their own right. The desire to stamp a mark to communicate meaning and even identity can be traced back to ancient times, suggestive of some deeper human need to extend something of ourselves symbolically.

The proceeding chapters have explored the potted history of brands and branding and examined key innovations, innovators, and challenges. We've hopefully helped you speak like a brand expert, with our chapter examining core concepts and debates. As you may appreciate, we have left a lot out, including much nuance. Although we have skipped over a detailed account of different types of brands, such as those within business-to-business contexts, or platform brands, luxury brands, serial brands, nation brands, and so on, we hope this guide will provide enough insight for you if you are operating in those sectors. Much of what we have covered is relatively universal across contexts, although the nature of a short guide (it's in the title after all) means deeper examination requires specialist texts.

When we wrote our textbook *Brand Management: Co-creating Meaningful Brands* (one last shameless plug), we took the view that an appreciation of co-creation did not necessarily negate previous research and practice. That is, we sought to integrate the body of knowledge on brand management to offer a more complete guide for the present and next generation of brand leaders or part-time brand managers. We take a similar approach here, selectively reviewing some core debates and contributions, and critically evaluating their claims. Although we do not believe in equivalence (like any business field there remains some extremely dodgy advice out there on brands), we do believe that there is the potential for more convergence in our understanding of brand management than the various camps, with their singular truths, would have us believe. Perhaps a grand theory of branding is possible after all.

The strength of our field lies in its pluralism (although too often we break into camps with high walls built around them), but also the cross-fertilization that comes from the interplay of academics and practitioners. This interaction needs to be strengthened particularly with the fragmentation of marketing and consumer research into almost separate domains. While marketing management research and practice regularly cross over, at the time of writing, consumer research is in danger of forgetting to offer usable insights, while practitioners are often locked into narrow models of human behavior that blind one to opportunities to add or even create value.

Knowledge of brands and branding continues to grow. Hopefully you realize the trajectory is not always (or even often) linear, but one made up of multiple pathways that sometimes diverge significantly, but which, in our view, should maybe cross over more often. Too often, advocates for one approach to brand building talk past each other, rather than seeking some common ground. This is understandable in a way. When you deal with issues of identity and differentiation, subconsciously you may have little choice to put distance between your approach and that of others. Since relevance is always key as long as its framed in familiar ways, creative reframing of your model, even when it is often not too dissimilar from what has preceded before is perhaps essential, particularly when you have an audience often susceptible to the appeal of the new.

We'd like to end with an appeal to wannabe brand gurus to embrace the logic of brand management when offering your latest new thing. Take comfort in knowing you won't have the full answer to brand building. Whatever data you have is always subject to limitations and assumptions (that usually help make your models elegant, but only if you leave out the messiness that comes with human behavior). While you may need to stress your points of difference, understanding and new insights may also come from realizing what you share as points of parity. Your new model may in reality just be an extension of some parent theory, that helps add value to what you do. Or, your insights or models may just be part of an arsenal, or architecture of brand tools, which may help organizations and consumers achieve particular jobs or outcomes.

Finally, remember while this book is at an end, the actual book on brand management should never be closed. Definitions will be and indeed need to be revised, reassessed, and sometimes thrown out. Changes in consumption practice will open up new scope for branding. Ethical issues, future pandemics, zombie hordes, alien invasions, ape risings, and the impact of climate change will present greater challenges for a model based on consuming more and more (something the advocates of access-based platform brands with their assumptions of decoupling consumption from sustainability have found out). In fact, greater attention to the necessary ecosystem for resilient brands is required, with lessons still needing to be learned from the COVID-19 pandemic. Advances in customer research and technology, along with external challenges, have the potential to extend, qualify, or even challenge what we have written here. We wouldn't have it any other way, and in that spirit, perhaps this book itself can become a serial brand (although only if the good people at Sage improve our rider).

References

Aaker, David A. (1991), *Managing Brand Equity*, The Free Press, New York.

Aaker, David A. (1996), *Building Strong Brands*, Simon & Schuster, New York.

Aaker, David A. (2012), "Win the Brand Relevance Battle and Then Build Competitor Barriers," *California Management Review*, 54(2), 43–57.

Aaker, David (2018), *Creating Signature Stories: Strategic Messaging that Energizes, Persuades and Inspires*, Morgan James Publishing, Virginia.

Aaker, David (2022), *The Future of Purpose-Driven Branding*, Morgan James, New York.

Aaker, David and Erich Joachimsthaler (2000), "The Brand Relationship Spectrum: The Key to the Brand Architecture Challenge," *California Management Review*, 42(4), 8–23.

Aaker, David and Erich Joachimsthaler (2000), *Brand Leadership*, Simon & Schuster, London.

Aaker, Jennifer L. (1997), "Dimensions of Brand Personality," *Journal of Marketing Research*, 34(3), 347–356.

Ahuvia, Aaron and Elif Izberk-Bilgin (2011), "Limits of the McDonaldization Thesis: eBayization and Ascendant Trends in Post-Industrial Consumer Culture," *Consumption Markets & Culture*, 14(4), 361–384.

Arnould, Eric J. and Craig J. Thompson (2005), "Consumer Culture Theory (CCT): Twenty Years of Research," *Journal of Consumer Research*, 31(4), 868–882.

Arsel, Zeynep and Craig J. Thompson (2011), "Demythologizing Consumption Practices: How Consumers Protect Their Field-Dependent Identity Investments from Devaluing Marketplace Myths," *Journal of Consumer Research*, 37(5), 791–806.

Arvidsson, Adam and Nicolai Peitersen (2013), *The Ethical Economy: Rebuilding Value after the Crisis*, Columbia University Press, New York.

Bardhi, Fleura and Giana M. Eckhardt (2017). "Liquid Consumption," *Journal of Consumer Research*, 44(3), 582–597.

Barry, Max (2003), *Jennifer Government*, Doubleday, Melbourne.

Barwise, Patrick (1993), "Brand Equity, Snark or Boojum?" *International Journal of Research in Marketing*, 10(1), 93–101.

Bedbury, Scott (2002), *A New Brand World: Eight Principles for Achieving Brand Leadership in the Twenty-First Century*, Penguin Group, New York.

Becker, Marin, Nico Wiegand and Werner J. Reinartz, (2019), "Does It Pay to Be Real? Understanding Authenticity in TV Advertising," *Journal of Marketing*, 83(1), 24–50.

Belk, Russell W., Melanie Wallendorf and John F. Sherry (1989), "The Sacred and the Profane in Consumer Behavior: Theodicy on the Odyssey," *Journal of Consumer Research*, 16(1), 1–38.

Beverland, Michael B. (2005), "Crafting Brand Authenticity: The Case of Luxury Wine," *Journal of Management Studies*, 42(5), 1003–1029.

Beverland, Michael B. (2009), *Building Brand Authenticity: 7 Habits of Iconic Brands*, Palgrave Macmillan, Basingstoke.

Beverland, Michael B. and Pinar Cankurtaran (2024), *Brand Management: Co-creating Meaningful Brands*, SAGE, London.

Beverland, Michael B. and Michael T. Ewing (2005), "Slowing the Adoption and Diffusion Process to Enhance Brand Repositioning: The Consumer Driven Repositioning of Dunlop Volley," *Business Horizons*, 48(September–October), 385–391.

Beverland, Michael B. and Francis J. Farrelly (2010), "The Quest for Authenticity in Consumption: Consumers' Purposive Choice of Authentic Cues to Shape Experienced Outcomes," *Journal of Consumer Research*, 36(5), 838–856.

Beverland, Michael B., Adam Lindgreen and Michiel W. Vink (2008), "Projecting Authenticity through Advertising: Consumer Judgments of Advertisers' Claims," *Journal of Advertising*, 37(1), 5–15.

Beverland, Michael B., Giana M. Eckhardt, Sean S. Sands, and Avi Shankar (2021), "How Brands Craft National Identity," *Journal of Consumer Research*, 48(4), 586–609.

Beverland, Michael B., Sarah J. S. Wilner and Pietro Micheli (2015), "Reconciling the Tension between Consistency and Relevance: Design Thinking as a Mechanism for Achieving Brand Ambidexterity," *Journal of the Academy of Marketing Science*, 43(5), 589–609.

Beverland, Michael B., Steven M. Kates, Adam Lindgreen, and Emily Chung (2010), "Exploring Consumer Conflict in Service Encounters," *Journal of the Academy of Marketing Science*, 83, 617–633.

Beverland, Michael, Pinar Cankurtaran and Leila Loussaïef (2022), "A Critical Framework for Examining Sustainability Claims of the Sharing Economy: Exploring the Tensions within Platform Brand Discourses," *Journal of Macromarketing*, 42(2), 214–230.

Binet, Les and Peter Field (2013), *The Long and the Short of It: Balancing Short and Long-Term Marketing Strategies*, Institute of Practitioners in Advertising, London.

Booker, Christopher (2004), *The Seven Basic Plots: Why We Tell Stories*, Bloomsbury, London.

Brown, Stephen (2016), *Brands and Branding*, SAGE, London.

Brown, Stephen, Robert V. Kozinets and John F. Sherry Jr. (2003), "Teaching Old Brands New Tricks: Retro Branding and the Revival of Brand Meaning," *Journal of Marketing*, 67(3), 19–33.

Brunk, Katarina H., Markus Giesler and Benjamin Hartman (2018), "Creating a Consumable Past: How Memory Making Shapes Marketization," *Journal of Consumer Research*, 44(6), 1325–1342.

Buell, Ryan W. and Andrew Otazo (2016), *IDEO: Human-Centered Service Design*, Harvard Business School Case 9-615-022, Cambridge, MA

Canniford, Robin (2011), "How to Manage Consumer Tribes," *Journal of Strategic Marketing*, 19(7), 591–606.

Cayla, Julien and Giana M. Eckhardt (2008), "Asian Brands and the Shaping of a Transnational Imagined Community," *Journal of Consumer Research*, 35(2), 216–230.

Christensen, Clayton M., Taddy Hall, Karen Dillon, and David S. Duncan (2016), "Know Your Customers' 'Jobs to Be Done'," *Harvard Business Review*, 94(9), 54–60.

Chung, Emily, Francis Farrelly, Michael B. Beverland, & Ingo O. Karpen (2018), "Loyalty or Liability: Resolving the Consumer Fanaticism Paradox," *Marketing Theory*, 18(1), 3–30.

Coupland, Jennifer C. (2005), "Invisible Brands: An Ethnography of Households and the Brands in Their Kitchen Pantries," *Journal of Consumer Research*, 32(1), 106–118.

Deal, Terrence E. and Allan A. Kennedy (1982) *Corporate Cultures: The Rites and Rituals of Corporate Life*, Addison Wesley Publishing, Reading.

Deighton, John (1999), *Snapple*, Harvard Business School Case, Cambridge, MA, pp. 599–126.

Dong, Lily and Kelly Tian (2009), "The Use of Western Brands in Asserting Chinese National Identity," *Journal of Consumer Research*, 36(3), 504–523.

Edwards, Helen (2018), "Is There Any Such Thing as Brand Love?" in Wiemer Snijders (ed.), *Eat Your Greens*, Matador, Leicestershire, pp. 190–201.

Edwards, Helen (2023), *From Marginal to Mainstream: Why Tomorrow's Brand Growth Will Come from the Fringes and How to Get Their First*, Kogan Page, London.

Firat, A. Fuat and Alladi Venkatesh (1995), "Liberatory Postmodernism and the Reenchantment of Consumption," *Journal of Consumer Research*, 22(3), 239–267.

Florida, Richard (2002), *The Rise of the Creative Class*, Basic Books, New York.

Foucault, Michel (1977), *Discipline and Punish*, Pantheon Books, New York.

Fournier, Susan (1998), "Consumers and Their Brands: Developing Relationship Theory in Consumer Research," *Journal of Consumer Research*, 24(4), 343–373.

Fournier, Susan (2012), *Diversity of Consumers' Relationships with Brands*. www.youtube.com/watch?v=63K2I1Q7WRY (accessed 1/5/2024).

Fournier, Susan and Giana M. Eckhardt (2019), "Putting the Person Back into Person-Brands: Understanding and Managing the Two-Bodied Brand," *Journal of Marketing Research*, 56(4), 602–619.

Fournier, Susan and Lara Lee (2009), "Getting Brand Communities Right," *Harvard Business Review*, 87(4), 105–111.

Fournier, Susan and David Glenn Mick (1999), "Rediscovering Satisfaction," *Journal of Marketing*, 63(4), 5-23.

Friedman, Thomas L. (1999), *The Lexus and the Olive Tree: Understanding Globalization*, Farrar, Strauss & Giroux, New York.

Giesler, Markus (2012), "How Doppelgänger Brand Images Influence the Market Creation Process: Longitudinal Insights from the Rise of Botox Cosmetic," *Journal of Marketing*, 76(6), 55–68.

Giesler, Markus and Ela Veresiu (2014), "Creating the Responsible Consumer: Moralistic Governance Regimes and Consumer Subjectivity," *Journal of Consumer Research*, 41(3), 840–857.

Gobé, Marc (2007), *Brand Jam: Humanizing Brands through Emotional Design*, Allworth Press, New York.

Gobé, Marc (2010), *Citizen Brand: 10 Commandments for Transforming Brands in a Consumer Democracy*, Allworth Press, New York.

Goodhardt Gerald J., Andrew Ehrenberg and Chris Chatfield (1984), "The Dirichlet: A Comprehensive Model of Buying Behaviour," *Journal of the Royal Statistical Society: Series A*, 147, 621–655.

Grayson, Kent and Radan Martinec (2004), "Consumer Perceptions of Iconicity and Indexicality and Their Influence on Assessments of Authentic Market Offerings," *Journal of Consumer Research*, 31(2), 296–312.

Grégoire, Yany, Thomas M. Tripp and Renaud Legoux (2009), "When Customer Love Turns into Lasting Hate: The Effects of Relationship Strength and Time on Customer Revenge and Avoidance," *Journal of Marketing*, 73(6), 18–32.

Grigorian, Vadim and Pierre Chandon (2010), *Diesel for Successful Living: Branding Strategies for an Up-Market Line Extension in the Fashion Industry*, The Case Centre, Cranfield University, UK, J504-007-1.

Guardian staff and agency (2024), "Hermés Sued in California Over Claims It Only Sells Birkins to 'Worthy' Customers," *The Guardian*. https://www.theguardian.com/fashion/2024/mar/20/hermes-birkin-handbag-lawsuit (accessed March 20, 2024).

Hatch, Mary Jo and Majken Schultz (2001), "Are the Strategic Stars Aligned for Your Corporate Brand?" *Harvard Business Review*, 79(February), 128–134.

Hatch, Mary Jo and Majken Schultz (2008), *Taking Brand Initiative: How Companies Can Align Strategy, Culture, and Identity through Corporate Branding*, John Wiley & Sons, London.

Hatch, Mary Jo and Majken Schultz (2017), "Toward a Theory of Using History Authentically: Historicizing in the Carlsberg Group," *Administrative Science Quarterly*, 62(4), 657–697.

Heath, Robert (2001), *The Hidden Power of Advertising*, NTC Publications, Bath.

Heath, Robert (2012), *Seducing the Subconscious: The Psychology of Emotional Influence in Advertising*, Wiley-Blackwell, London.

Heeris Christensen, Anna-Bertha, Richard Gyrd-Jones, and Michael B. Beverland (2024), "Dialectical Emotional Labour in Digital Person-Branding: The Case of Digital Influencers," *Organization Studies*, 45(4), 571–591.

Heller, Stephen (2008), *Iron Fists: Branding the 20th Century Totalitarian State*, Phaidon Press, London.

Hirsch, Paul M. and Daniel Z. Levin (1999), "Umbrella Advocates versus Validity Police: A Life-Cycle Model," *Organization Science*, 10(2), 199–212.

Holt, Douglas B. (1998), "Does Cultural Capital Structure American Consumption?" *Journal of Consumer Research*, 25(1), 1–25.

Holt, Douglas B. (2002), "Why Do Brands Cause Trouble? A Dialectical Theory of Consumer Culture and Branding," *Journal of Consumer Research*, 29(1), 70–90.

Holt, Douglas B. (2004), *How Brands Become Icons: The Principles of Cultural Branding*, Harvard Business School Press, Cambridge, MA.

Holt, Douglas B. and Douglas Cameron (2010), *Cultural Strategy: Using Innovative Ideologies to Build Breakthrough Brands*, Oxford University Press, Oxford.

Ind, Nicholas (2014), "Living the Brand," in Kartikeya Kompella (ed.), *The Definitive Book of Branding*, SAGE, London, pp. 199–218.

Izberk-Bilgin, Elif (2012), "Infidel Brands: Unveiling Alternative Meanings of Global Brands at the Nexus of Globalization, Consumer Culture, and Islamism," *Journal of Consumer Research*, 39(4), 663–687.

Jaffe, Joseph (2007), *Join the Conversation: How to Engage Marketing-Weary Consumers with the Power of Community, Dialogue, and Partnership*, Wiley, Melbourne.

Jones, John Philip (1998), *How Advertising Works: The Role of Research*, SAGE, London.

Kapferer, Jean Noël (2012), *The New Strategic Brand Management: Advanced Insights & Strategic Thinking*, Kogan Page, New York.

Kates, Steven M. (2004), "The Dynamics of Brand Legitimacy: An Interpretive Study in the Gay Men's Community," *Journal of Consumer Research*, 31(2), 455–464.

Keller, Kevin L. (1993), "Conceptualizing, Measuring, and Managing Customer-Based Brand Equity," *Journal of Marketing*, 57(January), 1–22.

Keller, Kevin L. (2003), *Strategic Brand Management*, Pearson Education, London.

Keller, Kevin L. (2023), "The Future of Brands and Branding: An Essay on Multiplicity, Heterogeneity, and Integration," *Journal of Consumer Research*, 48(4), 527–540.

Keller, Kevin L., Brian Sternthal and Alice Tybout (2002), "Three Questions You Need to Ask about Your Brand," *Harvard Business Review*, 80(9), 80–89.

Kim, W. Chan and Renee Mauborgne (2015), *Blue Ocean Strategy: How to Create Uncontested Market Space and Make the Competition Irrelevant*, Harvard Business School Press, Cambridge, MA.

Klein, Naomi (2000), *No Logo*, Fourth Estate, New York.

Lehman, David W., Kieran O'Connor, Balázs Kovács and George E. Newman (2019), "Authenticity," *The Academy of Management Annals*, 13(1), 1–42.

Levy, Sidney J. (1959), "Symbols for Sale," *Harvard Business Review*, July–August, 117–124.

Liaukonyte, Jura, Anna Tuchman and Xinrong Zhu (2023), "Do Boycotts and "Buycotts" Make a Difference?" *Harvard Business Review*, 101(3–4), 24.

Low, George S. and Ronald A. Fullerton (1994), "Brands, Brand Management, and the Brand Manager System: A Critical-Historical Evaluation," *Journal of Marketing Research*, 21(May), 173–190.

Luedicke, Marius K. (2015), "Indigenes' Responses to Immigrants' Consumer Acculturation: A Relational Configuration Analysis," *Journal of Consumer Research*, 42(1), 109–129.

Macintosh, Gerrard and Lawrence S. Lockshin (1997), "Retail Relationships and Store Loyalty: A Multi-Level Perspective," *International Journal of Research in Marketing*, 14(5), 487–497.

McCracken, Grant (1989), "Who Is the Celebrity Endorser? Cultural Foundations of the Endorsement Process," *Journal of Consumer Research*, 16(3), 310–321.

McCracken, Grant (2010), *Chief Culture Officer: How to Create a Living Breathing Corporation*, Basic Books, New York.

Merz, Michael A., Yi He and Stephen L. Vargo (2009), "The Evolving Brand Logic: A Service-Dominant Logic Perspective," *Journal of the Academy of Marketing Science*, 37(3), 328–344.

Miles, Sandra J. and W. Glynn Mangold (2005), "Positioning Southwest Airlines through Employee Branding," *Business Horizons*, 48(6), 535–545.

Mintzberg, Henry and James A. Waters (1985), "Of Strategies, Deliberate and Emergent," *Strategic Management Journal*, 6(3), 257–272.

Moore, Karl and Susan Reid (2008), "The Birth of the Brand: 4000 Years of Branding," *Business History*, 50(4), 419–432.

Morhart, Felicitas, Lucia Malär, Amélie Guèvremont, Florent Girardin and Bianca Grohmann (2015), "Brand Authenticity: An Integrative Framework and Measurement Scale," *Journal of Consumer Psychology*, 25(2), 200–218.

Moulard, Julie G., Randal D. Raggio and Judith A. G. Folse (2021), "Disentangling the Meanings of Brand Authenticity: The Entity-Referent Correspondence Framework of Authenticity," *Journal of the Academy of Marketing Science*, 49, 96–118.

Neumeier, Marty (2005), *The Brand Gap: How to Bridge the Distance between Business Strategy and Design*, New Riders, San Francisco, CA.

Nussbaum, Bruce (2011), "*Design Thinking Is a Failed Experiment, So What's Next?*" Fast Company, https://www.fastcompany.com/1663558/design-thinking-is-a-failed-experiment-so-whats-next (accessed 1/5/2024).

Olins, Wally (1978), *The Corporate Personality: An Inquiry into the Nature of Corporate Identity*, Mayflower Books, New York.

Packard, Vance (1957), *Hidden Persuaders*, David McKay, New York.

Penrose, Noel and Martin Moorhouse (1989), "The Valuation of Brands," *Marketing Intelligence & Planning*, 7(11/12), 30–33.

Peters, Tom (1997), *The Brand Called You*, Fast Company, August 31. www.fastcompany.com/28905/brand-called-you (accessed May 1, 2024).

Petty, Ross D. (2011), "The Codevelopment of Trademark Law and the Concept of Brand Marketing in the United States before 1946," *Journal of Macromarketing*, 31(1), 85–99.

Pine, B. Joseph and James H. Gilmore (1998), "Welcome to the Experience Economy," *Harvard Business Review*, July–August, 97–105.

Power, Michael (1992) "The Politics of Brand Accounting in the United Kingdom," *European Accounting Review* 1(1), 39–68.

Preece, Chloe, Finola Kerrigan and Daragh O'Reilly (2019), "License to Assemble: Theorizing Brand Longevity," *Journal of Consumer Research*, 46(2), 330–350.

Puntoni, Stefano, Jonathan Schroeder and Mark Ritson (2010), "Meaning Matters: Polysemy in Advertising," *Journal of Advertising*, 39(2), 51–64.

Rahinel, Ryan, Ashley S. Otto, Daniel M. Grossman and Joshua J. Clarkson (2021), "Exposure to Brands Makes Preferential Decisions Easier," *Journal of Consumer Research*, 48(4) 541–561.

Ries, Al and Jack Trout (1981), *Positioning: The Battle for Your Mind*, McGraw Hill, New York.

Ritson, Mark (2020a), "It's Time for Share of Search to Replace Share of Voice," *Marketing Week*. https://www.marketingweek.com/mark-ritson-share-of-search-share-of-voice/ (accessed May 1, 2024).

Ritson, Mark (2020b), "If 'Black Lives Matter' to Brands, where Are Your Black Board Members?" *Marketing Week*. https://www.marketingweek.com/mark-ritson-black-lives-matter-brands/ (accessed May 1, 2024).

Ritzer, George (1983), *The McDonaldization of Society*, SAGE, Newbury Park, CA.

Roberts, Kevin (2004), *Lovemarks: The Future beyond Brands*, Powerhouse Books, New York.

Rodas, Maria A., Deborah Roedder John and Carlos J. Torelli (2021), "Building Brands for the Emerging Bicultural Market: The Appeal of Paradox Brands," *Journal of Consumer Research*, 48(4), 633–650.

Romaniuk, Jenni (2018), *Building Distinctive Brand Assets*, Oxford University Press, Oxford.

Rose, Randall L. and Stacy L. Wood (2005), "Paradox and the Consumption of Authenticity through Reality Television," *Journal of Consumer Research*, 32(2), 284–296.

Russell, Cristel A. and Hope J. Schau (2014), "When Narrative Brands End: The Impact of Narrative Closure and Consumption Sociality on

Loss Accommodation," *Journal of Consumer Research*, 40(6), 1039–1062.

Rust, Roland T., Valerie A., Zeithaml and Kathleen N. Lemon (2004), "Customer-centered Brand Management," *Harvard Business Review*, 82(9), 110–120.

Schau, Hope J., Albert M. Muñiz, Jr. and Eric J. Arnould (2009), "How Brand Community Practices Create Value," *Journal of Marketing*, 73(5), 30–51.

Schouten, John W. and James H. McAlexander (1995), "Subcultures of Consumption: An Ethnography of the New Bikers," *Journal of Consumer Research*, 22(1), 43–61.

Sharifonnasabi, Zahra, Fleura Bardhi and Marius K. Luedicke (2020), "How Globalization Affects Consumers: Insights from 30 Years of CCT Globalization Research," *Marketing Theory*, 20(3), 273–298.

Sharp, Byron (2010), *How Brands Grow: What Marketers Don't Know*, Oxford University Press, Oxford.

Silver, Ike, Newman George and Deborah A. Small (2021), "Inauthenticity Aversion: Moral Reactance toward Tainted Actors, Actions, and Objects," *Consumer Psychology Review*, 4, 70–82.

Spicer, André, Pinar Cankurtaran, and Michael B. Beverland (2022), "Take a Look at Me Now: Consecration and the Phil Collins Effect," Cattani, G., Deichmann, D. and Ferriani, S. (Eds), *The Generation, Recognition and Legitimation of Novelty (Research in the Sociology of Organizations*, Vol. 77), Emerald Publishing Limited, Leeds, pp. 253–282.

Spiggle, Susan, Hang T. Nguyen and Mary Caravella (2012), "More Than Fit: Brand Extension Authenticity," *Journal of Marketing Research*, 49(6), 967–983.

Stengel, Jim (2011), *Grow: How Ideals Power Growth and Profit at the World's Greatest Companies*, Crown Publishing, New York.

Trout, Jack and Steve Rivkin (2009), *Repositioning: Marketing in an Era of Competition, Change, and Crisis*, McGraw Hill, New York.

Van Laer, Tom, Ko De Ruyter, Luca M. Visconti and Martin Wetzels (2014), "The Extended Transportation-Imagery Model: A Meta-Analysis of the Antecedents and Consequences of Consumers' Narrative Transportation," *Journal of Consumer Research*, 40(5), 797–817.

Vann, Elizabeth F. (2006), "The Limits of Authenticity in Vietnamese Consumer Markets," *American Anthropologist*, 108(2), 286–296.

Vargo, Stephen and Robert V. Lusch (2004), "The Service-Dominant Logic of Marketing," *Journal of Marketing*, 68(1), 1–17.

Walker, Rob (2010), *Buying in: The Secret Dialogue between What We Buy and Who We Are*, Random House, New York.

Whyte, William H. (1956), *The Organization Man*, Simon & Schuster, New York.

Wiertz, Caroline and Daniel Korschun (2021), "Cass Bayes Business School: Rebranding Due to Slavery Links," *NIM Marketing Intelligence Review*, 13(2), 56–61.

Wipperfürth, Alex (2005), *Brand Hijack: Marketing without Marketing*, Portfolio, New York.

Zaltman, Gerald (2003), *How Customers Think: Essential Insights into the Mind of the Market*, Harvard Business School Press, Cambridge, MA.

INDEX

A
Aaker, David, 11–12, 15, 20, 22–23, 33, 69, 71, 102
Aaker, Jennifer, 21
Apple, 6, 10, 16, 50, 63, 77, 94, 114–118
The Apprentice, 10
Authentic extensions, 33

B
Barwise, Patrick, 42
Bass, Frank, 36
Bateman, Patrick, 66
Belk, Russell, 23
Boaty McBoatface, 82
Body Shop, 12, 56, 99
Brand
  ambidexterity, 89–91
  and the self, 24
  archetypes, 22, 109
  architecture, 13, 23, 68–69, 98
  assets, 77
  audits, 55–57
  authenticity, 72–76, 85, 107–108
  awareness, 65
  bureaucracy, 32, 88
  business to business (B2B), 115–116
  celebrity brands, 9
  communities, 25–26
  consistency, 87–91
  corporate brands, 16
  defined, 11
  distinction, 50, 52
  doppelgänger, 118–119
  equity, 40–43
  extension, 33, 67–68
  global brands, 14, 103–109
  identity, 43–47, 61–62
  internal, 59–60
  invisible brands, 8
  logo, 76–79
  loyalty, 20–21, 38
  mantra, 59
  meaning, 80
  nation brand, 9
  obituary, 46
  person brands, 9
  personality, 21
  place, 109–110
  platform brands, 26, 82
  political branding, 8
  positioning, 45–46, 52
  purpose, 85–86, 101–103
  relationships, 26
  relevance, 87–91
  repositioning, 92, 95
  research, 61–64
  retail brands, 12
  retro brands, 7
  serial brands, 7, 110, 112
  tracking, 64–65
Brandr, 4
Brown, Stephen, 38
Brown, Tim, 83
Budweiser, 32, 46, 113
Burberry, 17

C
Cartman, Eric, 72
Cass Business School, 93
Channel equity, 41
Christensen, Clayton, 81–82
Co-creation, 81, 84
Coke, 12, 16, 27, 32, 61, 78, 98, 118
Consumer culture theory, 30–31
Counterfeiting, 107–108
Customer-based brand equity, 20–21
Customers jobs' to be done, 81–82

D
Design thinking, 50, 83, 90
Deterritorialization, 104–107
Diesel, 90–91
Differential effect, 41

Index

Dirichlet Model, 36
Dune, 96
Dunlop Volley, 100

E
eBayization, 103–104
Eckhardt, Giana, 9, 30
Edwards, Helen, 33–34, 54, 84
Effies, 34
Ehrenberg, Andrew, 35–37
Ehrenberg-Bass, 35–39, 47, 50, 53, 77–78, 87, 115
Emotional labor, 59
Employer brand equity, 41

F
FIFA, 30, 113
Florida, Richard, 57
Fournier, Susan, 9, 26–29, 83, 115
Fred Perry, 112–113
Friedman, Thomas, 104–105

G
Giesler, Markus, 89, 119
Gilmore, James, 49

H
Heath, Robert, 70–72
Hicks, Bill, 72, 114
Hijacks, 17
Hyperreality, 14
Hatch, Mary Jo, 15, 55, 60
Harley Davidson, 6, 16, 25, 32, 80
Holt, Douglas, 17, 31–32, 34, 46–47, 49–50, 80, 88–89, 93, 98–100, 115

I
IDEO, 83
Iittala, 78
Imagined community, 30
Influencer equity, 41
Intangible asset, 13
Interbrand, 42

J
Jones, John Philip, 86–87
J Walter Thompson, 21, 44

K
Kapferer, Jean Noël, 20
Kates, Steven, 99–100, 102–103
Keller, Kevin Lane, 20, 36, 38
Kendall Jenner, 98
KFC, 106–107
Klein, Naomi, 57, 75, 116
Kodak, 78, 94

L
L'Oréal, 28, 68
LEGO, 15, 60
Levy, Sid, 44
Love becomes hate effect, 28
LVMH, 13, 41, 95

M
Marketing funnel, 70
McAlexander, James, 25
McCracken, Grant, 98–99
McDonaldization, 103–104
McDonalds, 104, 118–119
Mental availability, 38
Mintzberg, Henry, 17
Martha Stewart, 9, 10
Marketing Science Institute, 20, 24

N
Neumeier, Marty, 33, 46, 65, 80
Nike, 20–21, 32, 49, 53, 77

O
Ogilvy, David, 86
Olins, Wally, 33, 44–45
Organization culture, 58–59

P
Patagonia, 102–103
Pepsi, 98–99
Peters, Tom, 10
Phil Collins Effect, 66
Pine, Joseph, 49
Point of difference, 48
Points of parity, 48
Proctor & Gamble, 19, 22, 68
Proto brands, 4

Q
Quaker Oats, 16

R
Reputation, 7
Ries, Al, 44
Ritson, Mark, 33, 45, 63, 102
Ritzer, George, 103
Roberts, Kevin, 29
Romaniuk, Jenni, 77–78
Rupert Murdoch, 19
Rust, Roland, 96

S
Saatchi & Saatchi, 29
Schouten, John, 25
Schultz, Majken, 15, 55, 60
Sciency, 32, 42, 120
Segmentation, 52–54, 62
Share of search, 63–64
Share of voice, 63–64
Sharp, Byron, 35–37, 110
Snapple, 16
Southwest Airlines, 56
Starbucks, 29, 118
Steinlager, 97
Steve Jobs, 9–10, 50

Storytelling, 70–72
Survivor, 71, 74

T
Thought world, 32, 88–89
Tik Tok, 40
Top of mind awareness, 65–66
Toyota, 23, 28, 51, 54, 112
Trappist beer, 75–76
Trout, Jack, 44, 92
Twilight, 51–52

U
Unilever, 19, 38, 68, 97, 101–102
Unique selling point (USP), 48, 52

V
Van Laer, Tom, 71
Vegemite, 82–83
Volvo, 51–52

Y
Yamaha Music, 60, 62, 95

Z
Zaltman Metaphor Elicitation Technique (ZMET), 62

www.ingramcontent.com/pod-product-compliance
Lightning Source LLC
LaVergne TN
LVHW011604060925
820435LV00022B/206